RIT - WALLACE LIBRARY
CIRCULATING LIBRARY BOOKS

OVERDUE FINES AND FEES FOR <u>ALL</u> BORROWERS

*Recalled = $1/ day overdue (no grace period)
*Billed = $10.00/ item when returned 4 or more weeks overdue
*Lost Items = replacement cost+$10 fee
*All materials must be returned or renewed by the duedate.

INTERNATIONAL FINANCE CORPORATION

DISCUSSION PAPER NUMBER 44

Trends in Private Investment in Developing Countries
Statistics for 1970-2000
and
the Impact on Private Investment of Corruption and the Quality of Public Investment

Stephen S. Everhart
Mariusz A. Sumlinski

The World Bank
Washington, D.C.

ISSN: 1012-8069 (IFC Discussion Papers)
ISBN: 0-8213-5010-2

Stephen S. Everhart is a Senior Economist and Mariusz A. Sumlinski is an Economist in the IFC Economics Department

Library of Congress Cataloging-in-Publication Data has been applied for.

Table of Contents

This twelfth annual edition of *Trends in Private Investment in Developing Countries* presents annual data on private and public investment for 63 developing countries. The report attempts to fill a gap in data collection and analysis. Information on the breakdown of total investment into its public and private components is not readily available from standard national account statistics. Where it may be available, the concept of public investment is not always precise. Most standard measures classify capital expenditures of state-owned enterprises as private investment. In contrast, the definition used here counts all investment undertaken by the public sector—including through state enterprises—as public sector investment. It is based on data compiled by the World Bank and IMF.

Guy Pfeffermann
Director, Economics Department
and Economic Adviser of the Corporation

The 2001 edition of *Trends in Private Investment in Developing Countries* continues the investigation of the relationship between public and private investment. The focus this year is on the quality of public investment, its interaction with corruption, and the resulting impact on private investment.

The first chapter provides descriptive statistics, reporting trends in private and public fixed investment in 63 developing countries. This year, coverage of the Eastern Europe and Central Asia Region has been substantially expanded. In addition, a few smaller economies have been added to the Latin America and the Caribbean sample.

On average, the ratio of private investment to GDP declined in 1999 from 15 percent to 14.1 percent of GDP compared to 1998, and from 16.2 percent to 15.7 percent in weighted average terms. Public investment increased from 7.3 percent to 7.5 percent of GDP in simple average terms, and remained at the 1998 level in weighted average terms. The 1999 decline brings investment ratios back to their 1995 level. Preliminary and incomplete estimates for the year 2000 suggest that private investment may be poised for a return to growth.

The second chapter examines whether higher levels of public investment are associated with higher or lower levels of private investment, the impact of corruption on this relationship, and the long-run implications for growth and sustainable development. The paper provides evidence consistent with the hypothesis that corruption lowers the quality of public investment and that this reduced quality of public investment is associated with lower private investment. These findings have important implications for policymakers and private investors. Policymakers have further evidence to justify anti-corruption campaigns in their countries. Private investors may use these findings to determine where the best opportunities are today—and as the business climate in emerging markets changes, where to invest tomorrow.

Chapter 1. Trends in Private and Public Investment

In 1999, the latest year for which national accounts data exist, private investment in the 60 countries included in the data set fell slightly below the 1998 level, in both average and in GDP weighted terms.[1] (For a discussion of the definitions, methods, and sources used in this publication, see appendix B.) Meanwhile, public investment increased slightly on average, but remained level in GDP weighted terms.[2] The ratio of average private investment to GDP fell to 14.1 percent (15.7 percent in GDP weighted terms) in 1999 (see figure 1.1). Public investment, on the other hand, increased on average to 7.5 percent of GDP from 7.3 percent in 1998 but remained at 8.2 percent of GDP in 1998-99 in GDP weighted terms (see figure 1.2).

Figure 1.1. Private Investment in Developing Countries, 1970-2000

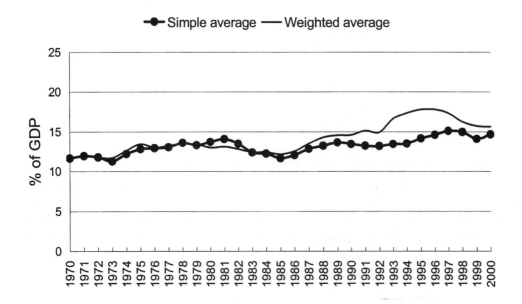

Note: This volume reports 2000 projections for about half the sample, which represents 50 percent of GDP of the full sample. These projections should be considered very preliminary and should be treated with caution. This document focuses on 1999 results.

---

[1] This volume reports 2000 projections for about half the sample, which represents 50 percent of GDP of the full sample. These projections should be considered very preliminary and thus should be treated with caution. This document focuses on 1999 results.

[2] Investment refers to gross domestic fixed investment, and encompasses both national and foreign from whatever finance source investment.

Figure 1.2. Public Investment in Developing Countries,
1970-2000

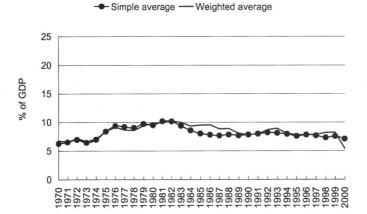

Note: This volume reports 2000 projections for about half the sample, which represents 50 percent of GDP of the full sample. These projections should be considered very preliminary and should be treated with caution. This document focuses on 1999 results.

Regional Trends

Regional trends mirrored the overall figures, with the exception of the Sub-Saharan Africa and Middle East and North Africa regions, as shown in figures 1.3 through 1.6. Most notably, it appears that East Asia is still suffering the aftershocks of the financial crisis which erupted in 1997, with private investment continuing to decline in 1999, both in average and GDP weighted terms and public investment declining as well in 1999. In Latin America and the Caribbean, South Asia, and Europe and Central Asia, private investment fell and public investment rose slightly in 1999.

Figure 1.3. Private Investment by Developing Region, 1970-2000
(weighted averages)

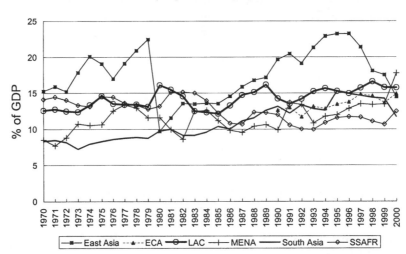

Figure 1.4. Private Investment by Developing Region, 1970-2000
(simple averages)

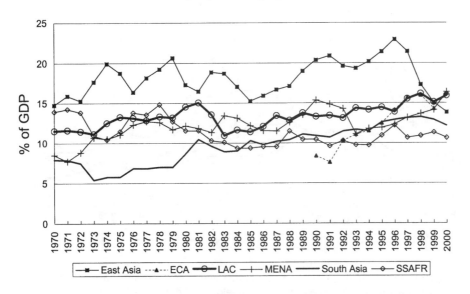

Latin America and the Caribbean (LAC). In 1998, Latin America and the Caribbean led all other regions in private investment growth. However, in 1999 the ratio of private investment to GDP fell by one percentage point, to 15.1 percent of GDP on average. The ratio of public investment to GDP went up by a half percentage point on average, and reached 7.2 percent of GDP in 1999. In GDP weighted terms, LAC's public investment figures were the lowest of all the regions in 1999, at 3.3 percent of GDP, down by almost half a percentage point from 1998. The largest LAC economies in the sample reported declining private investment to GDP ratios. In Argentina, private investment as a share of GDP decreased by almost two percentage points, in Brazil by less than a half percentage point, in Chile and Colombia by more than four percentage points, and in Republica Bolivariana de Venezuela, by almost two percentage points. Mexico recorded an increase of more than half a percentage point. The balance of the LAC countries in the sample recorded modest increases in private investment as a share of GDP.

Figure 1.5. Public Investment by Developing Region, 1970-2000
(weighted averages)

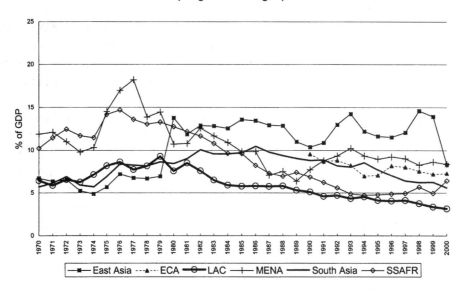

Figure 1.6. Public Investment by Developing Region, 1970-2000
(simple averages)

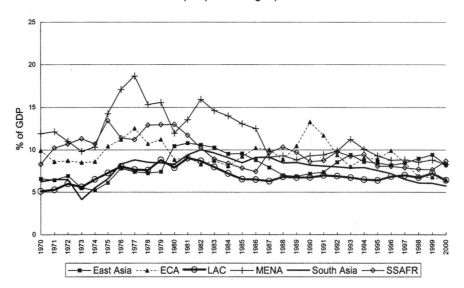

Sub-Saharan Africa. Private investment on average continued its moderate increasing trend for the third year in a row in 1999, reaching 11.3 percent of GDP. In GDP weighted terms, however, private investment declined slightly in 1999 to 10.6 percent of GDP from 11.1 percent in 1998. Public investment in Africa remained level in simple average terms and declined by almost one percentage point in weighted average terms. Private investment increased in Cote d'Ivoire and Mauritius, but remained flat or nearly flat in Benin, Guinea-Bissau, Madagascar and Seychelles. The remaining African countries covered in the data set recorded declines in private investment to GDP ratios.

4

South Asia. Private investment fell as a proportion of GDP in 1999, both in average and GDP weighted terms, but minimally. Nevertheless, private investment is expected to keep increasing in importance in this region, as it has done for more than 25 years. Private investment increased in Bangladesh, declined in India, and remained nearly flat in Pakistan. Public investment on average and in GDP weighted terms followed a declining trend as well, and remained at a level of about half of private investment.

   East Asia. The region's average private investment ratio declined in 1999 for the third year in a row to a level last recorded in 1985. The fall, however, was not as dramatic in GDP weighted terms. Not surprisingly, the most prominent declines in private investment were registered in the crisis countries: Indonesia, Republic of Korea, Malaysia, and the Philippines. Private investment increased in Cambodia but remained flat in China (although at a high level) and Thailand. Public investment increased only slightly on average and in GDP weighted terms. In 1999, East Asia had the highest average level of public investment to GDP among the regions, exceeding the global average by almost 2 percentage points.

   Eastern Europe and Central Asia (ECA). Private investment in 1999 declined on average to 14.3 percent of GDP from the high of 15.9 percent in 1998, declining in GDP weighted terms as well. The largest declines were recorded in Azerbaijan, Estonia, Turkey, and Uzbekistan. Bulgaria, Poland, and Romania reported increasing private investment to GDP ratios. Public investment in this region remained flat on average in 1999, at a level of 6.8 percent of GDP, declining slightly in GDP weighted terms.

   The Middle East and North Africa (MENA). Private investment increased slightly in 1999 to 14.1 percent of GDP on average. In GDP weighted terms, investment remained flat over 1998-99 period. Egypt and Morocco recorded increases in the private investment to GDP ratios, while Iran and Tunisia remained virtually flat. Public investment went up on average (in GDP weighted terms as well), to 8.8 percent of GDP.

   Individual country trends are shown in appendix C, along with the statistics.
Table 1.1 lists private investment ratios by country, listing them in descending order as of 1999 and comparing them to 1980 and 1990 (when data are available). Ratios for 2000 are also presented; as noted, these should be considered very preliminary and thus treated with caution.

Table 1.1. Private Investment in 1980, 1990, 1999 and 2000 (percent of GDP)				
	1980	1990	1999	2000
Grenada	6.9	25.8	28.8	28.8
Azerbaijan			28.2	23.6
Panama		7.4	26.3	26.4
Seychelles		14.8	24.8	17.3
Nicaragua		11.2	22.0	19.0
Korea, Republic of	25.5	32.2	22.0	
Mauritius	14.9	19.2	21.8	18.6
Estonia			21.4	23.1
Thailand	18.9	34.2	19.4	18.5
Dominican Republic	16.3	18.2	18.9	17.5
Mexico	13.9	13.6	18.9	18.6
St. Vincent		18.1	18.8	
Dominica		20.8	18.7	21.6
Morocco	11.8	16.4	17.3	16.0
China	3.7	8.3	17.0	
St. Lucia	25.1	13.8	16.9	15.8
Peru		12.9	16.8	17.0
Brazil	17.0	17.6	16.3	
Turkey	13.3	15.8	16.1	17.0
Argentina	19.2	9.4	16.1	15.4
Bangladesh	8.2	9.8	15.5	15.7
India	10.1	13.9	14.9	
Guatemala	10.5	10.4	14.8	14.0
Chile	11.2	18.4	14.5	16.4
Lithuania			14.3	
Paraguay	25.7	19.2	14.2	14.2
Trinidad & Tobago		10.7	14.2	16.3
Kazakhstan			14.0	
Tunisia	13.3	19.7	13.1	
Barbados	18.5	15.5	13.1	12.9
Egypt		16.7	13.0	14.0
El Salvador	6.4	11.2	13.0	13.0
Iran	11.4	8.5	13.0	19.0
Indonesia		19.5	12.9	
Philippines	18.8	18.9	12.9	12.2
Namibia	11.4	13.1	12.9	
Poland		8.5	12.7	12.8
Guyana		14.4	12.6	12.5
Belize	11.1	11.4	12.5	
Cote d'Ivoire		4.9	12.1	12.9
Bolivia		5.0	12.0	11.5
Yugoslavia, Federal R			11.4	13.1
Malaysia	19.5	20.9	11.3	10.8
Uruguay	11.9	8.3	10.6	12.1
Benin		6.0	10.6	11.3
South Africa	13.3	12.9	10.3	
Kenya	13.3	11.3	10.1	
Uzbekistan			9.7	7.5
Cambodia		8.8	9.6	
Venezuela, Rep.Boliv		4.9	8.8	8.4
Pakistan	7.7	8.9	8.3	8.6
Bulgaria		0.8	8.0	
Comoros		6.7	7.4	7.4
Romania			6.9	
Ecuador	14.1	12.4	6.9	15.4
Madagascar		6.9	6.8	8.2
Haiti		7.0	5.7	
Colombia	9.8	10.2	5.5	6.9
Guinea-Bissau		8.4	5.2	5.3
Malawi	4.7	8.6	2.2	4.1
Papua New Guinea		20.0		
Costa Rica	14.7	17.7		

6

Chapter 2. *Private Investment: the Impact of Corruption and the Quality of Public Investment*

This chapter focuses on the effects of corruption on public and private investment and their long-term implications for economic growth. Specifically, it raises the question whether corruption affects the quality of public investment and the level of private investment. Three fundamental questions are raised:

- is public investment associated with higher or lower private investment?
- does corruption influence this relationship? and
- what may be the long-term implications of these interactions for economic growth?

The chapter first reviews the literature exploring the impact of corruption on private investment. Section two explores the interaction effect between corruption and public investment, section three examines the linkages between private and public investment, section four presents our empirical analysis, and section five concludes.

I. *The Nature of Corruption and Its Effects on Private Investment*

Corruption is a pervasive and universal phenomenon. As witnessed throughout history, corruption can affect democratic and non-democratic countries, rich and poor countries, alike. In very recent times, corruption, or allegations of corruption of some sort, was instrumental in the reorganization of the political system in several countries.

There are many types of public corruption, including accepting bribes to shorten processing time, obtain monopoly power, or secure government procurement and contracts. Tanzi (1998) offers a common definition of corruption: the abuse of public power for private benefit.[3]

Research on corruption has expanded in recent years, yet work investigating its impact on *private* investment is still in its infancy. Mauro (1995) finds that an aggregate institutional indicator, a "corruption indicator," is negatively associated with aggregate investment in his sample of countries. Brunetti, Kisunko and Weder (1997) present results from a survey of entrepreneurs that suggest that perceived unreliability of the judiciary, government instability, and corruption negatively influence cross-country differences in aggregate investment. Brunetti and Weder (1997) find that among institutional factors, lack of rule of law, high corruption and real exchange rate distortions are the most detrimental for investment.

A number of recent studies have examined the impact of the business environment on investment. Pfeffermann, Kisunko, and Sumlinski (1999) investigated in a limited number of countries the link between private investment and perceived business obstacles in developing countries, obstacles such as corruption, unpredictability of the judiciary,

---

[3] Theobald (1990) provides a number of definitions of corruption.

onerous regulations for starting a business, tax and labor regulations, and others. Countries where these obstacles were perceived to be fewer had higher levels of private investment.

One reason why corruption seems to depress investment is that it acts as a tax on private investment.[4] A "corruption tax" is particularly burdensome for activities such as investment projects that by nature involve a long time horizon and a multiplicity of logistic, administrative and legal steps. Each of these steps is liable to incur corruption taxes, each cascading over the other. The result is an increase in the cost of capital, hence a reduction in anticipated profitability, as well as a relative incentive toward investments involving fewer administrative steps: that is, the tax is distorting, too.

Investigating the impact of corruption on private enterprise and public finance is not a new concept, yet quantifying the impact remains elusive.[5] A recent IMF note reports a survey by a resident representative in a CIS country suggesting that almost 40 percent of a new enterprise's expenses in the first year are "informal payments."[6] Forty percent is likely an extreme case, but table 2.1 below presents some results from a recent OECD/World Bank report that provides estimates of social losses for three eastern European countries.[7]

TABLE 2.1. CORRUPTION AND LOST REVENUE (PERCENT)

INDICATOR	ALBANIA	GEORGIA	LATVIA
Enterprises willing to pay higher taxes if corruption were eliminated	53	71	30
Additional taxes as a share of revenue that enterprises would be willing to pay if corruption were eliminated	11	22	15
Bribes typically paid as a share of firms' revenue	7	15	7

Source: Kaufmann, Pradhan, and Ryterman, (1998). Based on 1998 World Bank Surveys of 438 enterprise managers in Latvia (with Latvia Facts), 350 enterprise managers in Georgia (with GORBI), and 356 enterprise managers in Albania (with ACER).

One implication is that less corruption might translate into more resources available for private investment. In addition, strengthened public revenues as a result of less "leakage" due to corruption could translate into more public services and/or reduced taxes. Most important might be the impact on incentives: with high corruption, investment simply might not occur.

II. *Public Investment and Corruption: Is There an Interaction Effect?*

Tanzi and Davoodi (1997) investigate the impact of corruption on public investment, using infrastructure investment as their proxy for public investment and the

---

[4] See Shleifer and Vishny (1993) and Wei (1997).

[5] See Jain (2001) for a review.

[6] "Improving Governance and Fighting Corruption in the Baltic and CIS Countries," IMF Economic Issues Series, No. 21, 2000.

[7] These countries do not represent the extreme in commonly used index measures of corruption. Albania and Latvia are in the "moderate" range of the ICRG corruption index. Georgia is not rated.

Political Risk Service's *International Country Risk Guide* index as their measure of corruption. They find that corruption tends to increase the number of projects undertaken and to expand their size. Corruption increases the share of public investment to GDP, and also lowers the quality of public investment put in place.

The logic behind these findings is straightforward. Infrastructure projects can be large and the implementation is often carried out by private firms. The incentive for the private enterprise to pay a "commission" to secure the contract is strong, particularly when the contract is large. When the approval of investment projects is influenced by corrupt public officials, rates of return and cost-benefit analyses become mere exercises.

The firm paying the "commission" is unlikely to bear the cost of the bribe. It is more likely this cost will be recouped in some inefficient way. Perhaps project costs will be pared by adhering poorly to plan specifications or by using poor quality materials or workmanship. Perhaps an "understanding" will be reached with the bribed official that the initial low estimate will be revised upward as the project progresses. Or the bid may be padded initially. In the more rare instances of cost-plus contracting, the firm can hide the bribe expense through overpricing. All of these work to make the public investment in infrastructure more costly and less likely to meet specifications. [8]

We investigate the effect on private investment of possible interaction between corruption and public investment empirically in section four.

III. The Link Between Private and Public Investment

There is a growing consensus that private investment is more efficient and productive than public investment, yet the number of studies on the respective roles of private and public investment in *developing* economies is somewhat limited. Using relatively small sample sizes and limited time series, a number of studies have concluded that private investment has a larger positive impact on growth than public investment, among them, Khan and Reinhart (1990), Coutinho and Gallo (1991), and Serven and Solimano (1990).

Khan and Kumar (1997) expand the country coverage over previous works and examine a relatively long time period, 1970-1990. The authors find private and public investment both have a statistically significant positive association with growth. The magnitude differs considerably, however, with private investment having an estimated coefficient almost one-and-a half times as large as that of public investment.

Bouton and Sumlinski (2000) confirmed Khan and Kumar's results and found for a longer period an even larger coefficient on private investment and smaller coefficient on public investment. Thus, the degree of association of private investment with sustainable development and growth appears well established in the economics literature.

---

[8] Corruption appears to be particularly problematic in infrastructure investment, see Wade (1982) and Rose-Ackerman (1996).

A more difficult relationship to discern is that between public and private investment. Crowding-in of private investment by public investment is defined to occur when increased public investment is associated with increased private investment. This may arise because public infrastructure provision affects returns on private investment positively, hence enhancing the incentive to carry out such private investment. Crowding out occurs when the opposite is the case. A vast literature covers this subject, some recent works are presented in table 2.2 below. The table suggests that not only is there no consensus on the topic, but there are contradictory results, even for the same regions and countries.

TABLE 2.2. SELECTED LITERATURE REVIEW, CROWDING IN – CROWDING OUT

CITATION	SAMPLE COUNTRIES	FINDINGS
Oshikoya (1994)	African	For most countries in this sample, public investment in infrastructure is complementary to private sector investment
de Oliveira Cruz and Teixeira (1999)	Brazil	Private investment is crowded out by public investment in the short term, but in the long term these two variables are complements
Clements and Levy (1994)	Caribbean	Crowding out
Blejer and Khan (1984)	Developing	Government investment in infrastructure is complementary to private investment, other types of government investment are not
Balassa (1988)	Developing	Crowding out
Greene and Villanueva (1991)	Developing	Crowding in
Heng (1997)	Developing	Shows that public capital can crowd in private capital by raising the marginal productivity of labor and savings
Ghura and Goodwin (2000)	Developing	- Overall sample suggests crowding in - Public investment crowds in private investment in SSAFR, but crowds out in Asia and LAC
Shafik (1992)	Egypt	Effects of government policy on private investment are mixed, evidence of crowding out in credit markets and crowding in as a result of government investment in infrastructure
Sobhee (1999)	Mauritius	Empirics suggest expenditures on health and infrastructure stimulate private investment, expenditure on education does not
Nazmi and Ramirez (1997)	Mexico	Crowding out
Musalem (1989)	Mexico	Crowding in
Looney and Frederiken (1997)	Pakistan	Crowding in
Sakr (1993)	Pakistan	When government investment is disaggregated into infrastructure and non-infrastructure components, the latter crowds out private investment
Ahmed and Miller (2000)	OECD and Developing	- Government expenditure crowds out for both samples, plus pooled sample - For developing countries, government expenditure on transport and communication crowds in
Argimon, Gonzalez-Paramo, Alegre (1997)	OECD	Crowding in effect of private investment by public investment through the positive impact of infrastructure on private investment productivity
Monadjemi and Huh (1998)	OECD (Australia, UK, USA)	Empirics provide limited support for crowding out effects of government investment on private investment
Pereira and Flores de Frutos (1999)	USA	Crowding in
Pereira (2000)	USA	Crowding in
Pereira (2001)	USA	- At the aggregate level, public investment crowds in private investment - Disaggregating private investment shows that the crowding in effect of public investment is strong for equipment and only marginal for structures - Public investment marginally crowds out private investment in information equipment

11

A simple investigation of the relationship between public and private investment is presented in table 2.3 below, where the within-country correlations between public and private investment for all 63 countries in our sample are presented.[9]

The table shows that there is sometimes crowding out and sometimes crowding in, with an almost even split between the two. This may explain the contradictory findings in the literature (the studies summarized in table 2.2). And it is also important to note that in addition to the axiom "correlation does not prove causation," its corollary is "partial correlations are not necessarily preserved in a multi-variable framework." More rigorous testing is therefore presented in the next section.

---

[9] Periods for the correlations vary by country, ranging from the entire sample period of 1970-2000, to as brief as 1995-2000.

TABLE 2.3. INVESTMENT CORRELATIONS *denotes significance at 5% level

Region	Income	Country	Private vs. Public	
ECA	Lower middle	Bulgaria	-88%	*
ECA	Lower middle	Lithuania	-83%	
SSAFR	Low	Mauritania	-77%	*
ECA	Upper middle	Turkey	-76%	*
LAC	Lower middle	Bolivia	-74%	*
ECA	Low	Azerbaijan	-70%	
ECA	Upper middle	Poland	-70%	*
LAC	Upper middle	Grenada	-68%	*
LAC	Lower middle	St. Vincent	-66%	*
East Asia	Low	Indonesia	-62%	*
East Asia	Low	Cambodia	-61%	*
LAC	Upper middle	Mexico	-57%	*
ECA	Lower middle	Romania	-55%	
LAC	Upper middle	Chile	-55%	*
SSAFR	Low	Benin	-40%	
LAC	Lower middle	Belize	-39%	*
South Asia	Low	Pakistan	-36%	*
MENA	Lower middle	Morocco	-35%	
LAC	Lower middle	Paraguay	-34%	
ECA	Upper middle	Estonia	-32%	
LAC	Upper middle	Argentina	-31%	
SSAFR	Upper middle	Seychelles	-25%	
LAC	Upper middle	Dominica	-24%	
LAC	Upper middle	St. Lucia	-23%	
SSAFR	Lower middle	Namibia	-22%	
LAC	Upper middle	Brazil	-21%	
LAC	Lower middle	Colombia	-17%	
SSAFR	Low	Comoros	-17%	
LAC	Upper middle	Barbados	-17%	
LAC	Upper middle	Venezuela, R. B.	-15%	
LAC	Lower middle	Costa Rica	-14%	
LAC	Lower middle	Dominican Republic	-12%	
ECA	Lower middle	Kazakhstan	-5%	
SSAFR	Low	Madagascar	-4%	
South Asia	Low	India	-2%	
LAC	Lower middle	Ecuador	-2%	
LAC	Lower middle	El Salvador	1%	
MENA	Lower middle	Tunisia	4%	
East Asia	Upper middle	Korea, Rep. of	6%	
LAC	Upper middle	Uruguay	6%	
SSAFR	Low	Cote d'Ivoire	8%	
LAC	Lower middle	Guatemala	9%	
East Asia	Lower middle	Thailand	9%	
East Asia	Lower middle	Papua New Guinea	11%	
ECA	Low	Uzbekistan	15%	
MENA	Lower middle	Egypt	17%	
LAC	Upper middle	Trinidad & Tobago	20%	
LAC	Lower middle	Peru	23%	
East Asia	Lower middle	Philippines	24%	
SSAFR	Upper middle	Mauritius	25%	
East Asia	Upper middle	Malaysia	27%	
LAC	Lower middle	Guyana	37%	
SSAFR	Low	Kenya	38%	*
SSAFR	Low	Malawi	50%	*
LAC	Low	Haiti	51%	*
MENA	Lower middle	Iran	52%	*
SSAFR	Low	Guinea-Bissau	56%	*
East Asia	Low	China	59%	*
South Asia	Low	Bangladesh	64%	*
LAC	Lower middle	Panama	64%	*
LAC	Low	Nicaragua	67%	*
SSAFR	Upper middle	South Africa	78%	*
ECA	Lower middle	Yugoslavia, Fed. Rep.	97%	

13

IV. Econometric Analysis

This section presents the econometric investigation of the questions of interest for the study. First, we investigate the impact of corruption on public investment; then we continue our investigation of the "crowding-in vs. crowding-out" debate, focusing on the impact of corruption; we conclude this section with the possible long-run implications of the empirical findings of the first two subsections.

a) Impact of corruption on public investment

Following Tanzi and Davoodi (1997), we investigate the impact of corruption on public investment by tracing the impact of corruption on the quality of public infrastructure. We measure infrastructure quality through three proxies: paved roads in good condition as a percentage of total roads; electric power system losses as a percentage of total power output; and telephone faults per 100 mainlines per year.[10] A priori, if corruption leads to lower quality public investment, then in more corrupt countries we expect the percentage of paved roads to be lower, and the number of telephone faults and electrical system losses to be higher. The first two measures are available in the World Bank Development Indicators database. Telecommunications faults are from the International Telecommunications Union data base.

Our measure of corruption is from the Political Risk Service's *International Country Risk Guide*. This publication attempts to measure the phenomenon by investigating whether high ranking government officials are likely to demand special payments and if officials in lower levels of government generally expect illegal payments in the form of bribes connected with import-export licenses, exchange controls, tax assessment, police protection, or loans. The *ICRG* provides a numeric, time-series measure of corruption ranging from zero to six, with higher values indicating less corruption. Studies of corruption using this measure include Knack and Keefer (1995), Svensson (1998), and Tanzi and Davoodi (1997, 2000).

Regressing the corruption index on each of the proxies for quality of public investment yields econometric results consistent with Tanzi and Davoodi (1997). We are, however, using only *developing* country economies and cover a longer time period, 1970-1999. Our results are presented in table 2.4 below.[11] As expected, more corrupt countries have more telephone faults per 100 lines, more electrical system losses as a percentage of output, and a lower percentage of paved roads.

---

[10] These proxies are not perfect but they do provide some measure of the quality of public investment, further, a review of the literature reveals few alternative measures available for large numbers of developing countries.

[11] Tanzi and Davoodi also control for per capita GDP and find, unsurprisingly, that countries with higher per capita GDP tend to have better quality infrastructure. They present a number of other specifications and control variables, with mixed results.

TABLE 2.4. **THE EFFECT OF CORRUPTION ON QUALITY OF INFRASTRUCTURE**

Dependent variable	Telephone faults per 100 main lines	Roads, paved (% of all roads)	Electric power transmission and distribution losses (% of output)
Constant	129.6	20.2	19.8
	16.2	4.7	24.6
Corruption[a]	-17.1	4.8	-1.7
	-3.4	3.4	-6.7

Note: Shaded cells are t-statistics.
[a] Higher index indicates less corruption.

b) Crowding-in vs. crowding-out and the impact of corruption

In specifying a model to investigate the impact of public investment and corruption on private investment, a survey of the literature provided an array of techniques, possible control variables, and specifications.[12] After investigating of a number of specifications, the following model was selected:

Concept

I_p / GDP =

$(I_p$ / GDP$)_{-1}$	*lagged private investment to GDP*
Broad Money/GDP	*financial deepness, availability of credit*
External Debt/GDP	*debt overhang*
CAB/GDP	*external balance*
$(I_g$ / GDP$)$*Corruption	*interaction between corruption index, public investment*
I_g / GDP	*public investment to GDP: crowding in/out*
constant	*all other effects*

Lagged private investment is undoubtedly a significant component in current private investment, hence it is an obvious choice for the model. The next three variables: broad money to GDP, external debt to GDP, and the current account balance to GDP, are

---

[12] Considerable debate exists in the econometrics literature about the proper unbalanced panel data technique. As our interest lies more with the economics than the econometrics of the investigation, we have chosen to present the standard OLS, or pooled least squares estimates, as well as the random effects results (which are virtually the same). Hausman (1978) and Wu (1973) tests suggest random effects specification is indicated over fixed effects. The results of the Breusch—Pagan (1980) test for choice between OLS and random effects indicated OLS is the proper specification. For a review of issues in panel data estimation, see Arellano and Bover (1995), Ahmed and Miller (2000), Baltagi (1995), Bhargava and Sargan (1983), Boehmer and Megginson (1990), Cashel-Cordo and Craig (1990), Chang (1979), and Pesaran and Smith (1995).

included as control variables.[13] The variables of interest for our research are the interaction term between on one hand, public investment to GDP and the corruption index, and on the other, public investment to GDP. The full sample results are presented in table 2.5 below.

As one would expect, lagged private investment is highly significant. Its steadiness over time as a share of GDP virtually assures the significance. Broad money, our measure of the financial depth of the economy, is also significant. The debt overhang is also significant, with the expected negative sign. The significant negative coefficient on the current account balance is consistent with our expectations. A higher level of private investment is associated with an increased current account deficit (or a reduced surplus). Note that private FDI typically finances a large portion of the current account in emerging economies.

TABLE 2.5. PRIVATE INVESTMENT, CORRUPTION, AND CROWDING OUT : FULL SAMPLE RESULTS

Independent variable	Means	RE	PLS
Constant		1.548	1.704
		5.1	5.3
Private investment/GDP lagged	13.5	0.899	0.886
		54.0	50.0
Broad money/GDP	42.2	0.019	0.020
		3.3	3.4
External debt/GNP	81.8	-0.006	-0.006
		-4.7	-4.7
Current account balance/GDP	-4.5	-0.131	-0.137
		-6.1	-6.3
(Public inv./GDP)*Corruption[a]	7.8; 3.0	0.023	0.022
		2.2	2.0
Public investment/GDP	7.8	-0.156	-0.160
		-4.0	-3.9

RE – random effects estimation, PLS – pooled least squares estimation.
Note: Shaded cells are t-statistics.
[a] Higher index indicates less corruption.

The primary relationships of interest for this research, the interaction between public investment and corruption, and the measure of crowding-out vs. crowding in, are also significant and of the "correct" sign. The explanation is as follows:

We know from Tanzi and Davoodi (1997) that corruption is associated with poor quality public investment, consistent with our own results, summarized in table 2.4, and that it also inflates public investment levels. These effects are captured in our model by two variables. First, controlling for the other variables in the model above, a higher level of public investment is associated with a lower

---

[13] A review of the literature reveals numerous possible determinants of investment and possible control variables. Some authors have used institutional factors such as education or civil unrest as control variables but we have chosen to limit the variables to those we consider most germane for the questions of interest. Useful references include Bier (1992), Blejer and Kahn (1984), Bouton and Sumlinski (2000), Brunetti and Weder (1997), Cardoso (1993), Fischer (1991, 1993), Ghura and Goodwin (2000), Greene and Villanueva (1991), Larrain and Vergara (1993), Oshikoya (1994), Ozler and Rodrik (1992), Sakr (1993), Serven and Solimano (1992), and Solimano (1989).

level of private investment, i.e., crowding out. The negative relationship is statistically significant. Second, the interaction between the corruption index and the level of public investment captures the indirect effect of corruption via its impact on the quality of public investment. The coefficient on the (Public inv./GDP)*Corruption variable is positive and statistically significant. A larger value for the corruption index signifies less corruption, which implies that any given level of public investment will be of higher quality than it would be with higher corruption (a lower index). Less corruption leads to higher quality public investment, and this is associated with a higher level of private investment.

In summary, the evidence comes out in favor of the crowding out hypothesis, with the crowding out stronger in the presence of corruption. It is important to note, however, that due to data limitations, we were only able to work with figures for total public investment. Numerous studies[14] have shown that certain types of infrastructure and public investment facilitate both growth and private investment.

Table 2.6 below presents regional results. With the exception of Africa, all conclusions are similar to the overall sample discussion presented above. The positive coefficient on the interaction term for all regions *except* Africa suggests that public investment typically has a negative influence on private investment. Why then should African public investment be associated with a higher level of private investment (i.e., crowds-in)? One possible explanation is that the low initial endowment of capital means that the addition of any investment, regardless of quality, yields high returns.

---

[14] Easterly and Rebelo (1993) find that public investment in communication and transport infrastructure has a strong positive effect on growth. Infrastructure such as paved roads, telephone density per worker and adequate electricity generation have been found to have a strong effect on subsequent growth (Easterly and Levine 1997, Canning 1999, Canning and Bennathan 2000). Odedokun (1997) shows that in developing countries, public investment in infrastructure facilitates private investment and growth, whereas non-infrastructure public investment has the opposite effect.

TABLE 2.6. PRIVATE INVESTMENT, CORRUPTION, AND CROWDING OUT : REGIONAL RESULTS

Independent variable	Full Sample	LAC	ASIA	SSAFR	ECA	MENA
Constant	1.704	2.680	4.451	3.944	3.953	2.989
	5.3	4.7	4.6	1.2	1.7	1.4
Private investment/GDP lagged	0.886	0.807	0.886	0.098	0.865	0.694
	50.0	25.5	26.4	0.6	10.2	6.3
Broad money/GDP	0.020	0.023	0.022	0.165	-0.021	-0.002
	3.4	2.4	1.5	2.8	-0.6	-0.1
External debt/GNP	-0.006	-0.008	-0.034	-0.016	0.001	0.019
	-4.7	-4.4	-4.0	-2.0	0.1	1.5
Current account balance/GDP	-0.137	-0.183	-0.138	-0.061	0.089	-0.006
	-6.3	-5.7	-3.2	-0.9	0.8	-0.1
(Public inv./GDP)*Corruption	0.022	0.042	0.033	-0.190	0.022	0.018
	2.0	2.1	1.7	-1.8	0.5	0.2
Public investment/GDP	-0.160	-0.260	-0.323	0.695	-0.204	-0.069
	-3.9	-3.5	-3.0	2.6	-1.0	-0.3

Note: Shaded cells are t-statistics. Method of estimation: pooled least squares.

c) Long-run implications of the empirical findings

Of particular interest to policymakers and private investors are the long run consequences of their investment decisions. We find that in the full sample, public investment tends to crowd out private investment in the short-run analyses presented in tables 2.5 and 2.6. If the 'crowding-out in the presence of corruption' finding is correct, then estimates of the long-run *negative* impact of any increase in *public* investment on the level of *total* investment would provide additional ammunition for policy-makers intent on combating corruption.

We solve for long-run effects by performing a Koyck[15] transformation on equation (1) above, the details are provided in appendix A. This transformation changes the short-run effects of table 2.6 into the long-run effects presented in table 2.7 below. In table 2.7 the short-run effects of each variable from table 2.6 (full sample results) are presented above the Koyck-transformed, long-run effects.

---

[15] See Koyck (1954) and Evans (1969).

TABLE 2.7. PRIVATE INVESTMENT DYNAMICS: LONG- AND SHORT-RUN EFFECTS		
Independent Variable		**Full Sample**
Constant		1.704
Private investment/GDP lagged		0.886
Broad money/GDP	SR	0.020
	LR	0.178
External debt/GNP	SR	-0.006
	LR	-0.055
Current account balance/GDP	SR	-0.137
	LR	-1.203
(Public Inv./GDP)*Corruption	SR	0.022
	LR	*0.191*
Public investment/GDP	SR	-0.160
	LR	*-1.408*

TABLE 2.8. IMPACT ON PRIVATE INVESTMENT OF 1% POINT RISE IN PUBLIC INVESTMENT			
	Direct effect	**Indirect Effect via Interaction Term**	**Total Effect**
Long-Run Coefficient	*-1.408*	*0.191*	
Level of Corruption			
High (index=0)	-1.41	0.00	-1.41
Middle (index=3)	-1.41	0.57	-0.84
Low (index=6)	-1.41	1.14	-0.26

Table 2.8 and figure 2.1 present the long-run impact on private investment of a 1 percentage point rise in public investment. With high corruption, a 1 percentage point increase in public investment leads to a 1.41 percent decline in private investment, resulting in a 0.41 percent decline in *total* investment. When corruption is low, crowding out still occurs but the decline in private investment is only 0.26 percent of GDP. This value is, however, not statistically different from zero. Thus in an environment of low corruption, there may well be no crowding out.

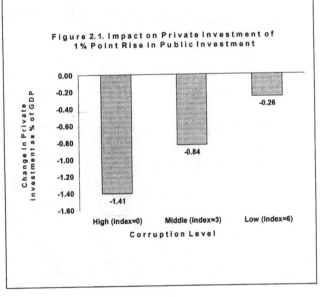

Figure 2.1. Impact on Private Investment of 1% Point Rise in Public Investment

V. Conclusions

This paper provides evidence consistent with the hypothesis that corruption lowers the quality of public investment, and this poor quality public investment is associated with lower private investment. The result is that if a highly corrupt country raises the level of public investment, the productivity of the new public investment put in place is low, and private investment falls. It also appears from the data that as this poor quality public investment is put in place, private investors are able to discern the difference and react by reducing their investment.

These findings have important implications for policymakers and private investors. Policymakers have further evidence to justify anti-corruption campaigns in their countries, as long-term growth depends on the flow of private investment, as well as on the flow of good quality public investment. Private investors may use these findings to determine where the better opportunities are today—and as the business climate changes in emerging markets, where to invest tomorrow.

References

Ahmed, Habib, and Stephen M. Miller. 2000. "Crowding-Out and Crowding-In Effects of the Components of Government Expenditure." *Contemporary Economic Policy* 18(1):124-33.

Arellano, M. and O. Bover. 1995. "Another Look at the Instrumental Variables Estimation of Error-Component Models." *Journal of Econometrics* 68(1)29-51.

Argimon, Isabel, Jose M. Gonzalez-Paramo, and Jose M. Roldan Alegre. 1997. "Evidence of Public Spending Crowding-Out From a Panel of OECD Countries." *Applied Economics* 29(8):1001-10.

Aschauer, D.A. 1989. "Does Public Capital Crowd Out Private Capital?" *Journal of Monetary Economics* 24(2):171-88.

———. 1989b. "Is Public Expenditure Productive?" *Journal of Monetary Economics* 23(2):177-200.

Balassa, Bela. 1988. "Public Finance and Economic Development." World Bank Working Paper No. 31. Washington, D.C.

Bardhan, Pranab. 1997. "Corruption and Development: A Review of Issues." *Journal of Economic Literature* 35(September):1320-46.

Baltagi, Badi H. 1995. *Econometric Analysis of Panel Data*. New York: Wiley.

Barro, Robert J. 1989. "A Cross Country Study of Growth, Saving and Government." NBER Working Paper, No. 2855. Cambridge, MA.

———. 1991. "Economic Growth in a Cross Section of Countries." *Quarterly Journal of Economics* 106 (2):407-43.

Beim, David and Charles Calomiris. 2000. *Emerging Financial Markets*. New York: McGraw-Hill.

Bhargava, A. and J.D. Sargan. 1983. "Estimating Dynamic Random Effects Models from Panel Data Covering Short Time Periods." *Econometrica*. 51(6):1635-59.

Bier, Willem. 1992. "Macroeconomic Models for the PC." IMF Working Paper:92/110. Washington, D.C.

Blejer, Mario, and Mohsin Khan. 1984. "Government Policy and Private Investment in Developing Countries." IMF Staff Papers 31, no. 2, pp. 379-403. Washington, D. C.

Boehmer, E. and W.L. Megginson. 1990. "Determinants of Secondary Market Prices for Developing Country Syndicated Loans." *The Journal of Finance* 45(5):1517-40.

Bouton, Lawrence and Mariusz A. Sumlinski. 2000. *Trends in Private Investment in Developing Countries. Statistics for 1970-1998*" IFC Discussion Paper 41. Washington , D.C.

Braguinsky, Serguey. 1996. "Corruption and Schumpeterian Growth in Different Economic Environments." *Contemporary Economic Policy* 14(July):14-25.

Breusch, T. S. and A. R. Pagan. 1980. "The Lagrange Multiplier Test and its Applications to Model Specification in Econometrics." *Review of Economic Studies* 47(1): 239-53.

Brunetti, Aymo and Beatrice Weder. 1997. *Investment and Institutional Uncertainty: A Comparative Study of Different Uncertainty Measures*. IFC Technical Paper 4. Washington, D.C.

Brunetti, Aymo, Gregory Kisunko, and Beatrice Weder. 1997. *How Businesses see government: Responses from Private Sector Surveys in sixty-nine Countries*. IFC Discussion Paper 33. Washington, D.C.

Canning, David. 1999. "Infrastructure's Contribution to Aggregate Output." Policy Research Working Paper 2246. World Bank, Policy Research Department. Washington, D.C.

Canning, David and Esra Bennathan. 2000. "The Social Rate of Return on Infrastructure Investments." Policy Research Working Paper 2390. World Bank, Policy Research Department. Washington, D.C.

Cardoso, E. 1993. "Macroeconomic Environment and Capital Formation in Latin America." In L. Serven and A. Solimano, eds. *Striving for Growth after Adjustment: The Role of Capital Formation*. Washington, D.C.: World Bank.

Cashel-Cordo, P. and S.G. Craig. 1990. "The Public Sector Impact of International Resource Transfers." *Journal of Development Economics* 32(1):17-42.

Chang, H. S. 1979. "A Study of Industry Location from Pooled Time-Series and Cross-Section Data: The Case of Cotton Textile Mills." *Quarterly Review of Economics and Business* 19(3):457-71.

Clements, Benedict, and Joaquim V. Levy. 1994. *Public Education Expenditure and Other Determinants of Private Investment in the Caribbean.*" IMF Working Paper 94/122. Washington, D.C.

Coutinho, Rui, and G. Gallo. 1991. "Do Public and Private Investment Stand in Each Other's Way." World Development Report background paper, mimeo. World Bank. Washington, D.C.

De Gregorio, J. 1991. "Economic Growth in Latin America." IMF Working Paper 71. Washington, D.C.

De Long, Bradford, and Lawrence Summers. 1993. "How Strongly Do Developing Economies Benefit From Equipment Investment?" *Journal of Monetary Economics* 32(December):395-415.

de Oliveira Cruz, Bruno, and Joanilio R. Teixeira. 1999. "The Impact of Public Investment on Private Investment in Brazil, 1947-1990." *CEPAL Review* 0(67):75-84.

Easterly, William and Ross Levine. 1997. "Africa's Growth Tragedy: Policies and Ethnic Divisions." *Quarterly Journal of Economics* 112(4):1203-50.

Easterly, William and Sergio Rebelo. 1993. "Fiscal Policy and Economic Growth: An Empirical Investigation." *Journal of Monetary Economics* 32(3):417-58.

Evans, Michael. 1969. *Macroeconomic Activity: Theory, Forecasting and Control*. New York: Harper & Row.

Fischer, S. 1991. "Growth, Macroeconomics, and Development." *NBER Macroeconomics Annual 1991:329-64*. London.

————. 1993. "The Role of Macroeconomic Factors in Growth." NBER Working Paper No. 4565. Cambridge, MA.

Friedman, Eric, Simon Johnson, Daniel Kaufmann and Pablo Zoido-Lobaton. 2000. "Dodging the Grabbing Hand: The Determinants of Unofficial Activity in 69 Countries." *Journal of Public Economics* 76(3):459-93.

Ghura, D. 1995. "Macro Policies, External Forces and Economic Growth in Sub-Saharan Africa." *Economic Development and Cultural Change*, 43(4): 759-78.

————. "Tax Revenue in Sub-Saharan Africa: Effects of Economic Policies and Corruption." IMF Working Paper 135. Washington, D.C.

Ghura, D. and Barry Goodwin. 2000. "Determinants of Private Investment: A Cross-Regional Empirical Investigation." *Applied Economics* 32(14):1819-29.

Ghura, D. and M.T. Hadjimichael. 1995. "Growth in Sub-Saharan Africa." IMF Working Paper 136. Washington, D.C.

Graziano, Luigi. 1980. *Clientelismo e Sistema Politico, Il Caso dell Italia*. Milan: F. Angeli.

Greene, Joshua, and Delano Villanueva. 1991. "Private Investment in Developing Countries: An Empirical Analysis." IMF Staff Papers 38(1):33-58. Washington, D.C.

Hausman, J. 1978. "Specification Tests in Econometrics." *Econometrica* 46(6):1251-71.

Heng, Tan Kim. 1997. "Public Capital and Crowding In." *Singapore Economic Review* 42(2):1-10.

Hindricks, Jean, Michael Keen, and Abinay Muthoo. 1999. "Corruption, Extortion, and Evasion." *Journal of Public Economics* 74(3):395-430.

Holtz-Eakin, D. 1994. "Public Sector Capital and the Productivity Puzzle." *Review of Economics and Statistics* 76(1):12-21.

Huntington, Samuel. 1968. *Political Order in Changing Societies*. New Haven: Yale University Press.

Ingram, Gregory, and Marianne Fay. 1994. Background paper for World Development Report 1994 – Infrastructure for Development. Washington, D.C., mimeo.

Jain, Arvind K. 2001. "Corruption: A Review." *Journal of Economic Surveys* 15 (1): 71-121.

Jaspersen, Frederick, Anthony Aylward, and Mariusz Sumlinski. 1995. "Trends in private investment for developing countries: statistics for 1970-1994." IFC Discussion Paper 28. Washington, D.C.

Johnson, Simon, Daniel Kaufmann, and Pablo Zoido-Lobatón. 1999. "Corruption, Public Finances, and the Unofficial Economy." Policy Research Working Paper 2169, World Bank, Policy Research Department. Washington, D.C.

Kaufmann, Daniel, Sanjay Pradhan, and Randi Ryterman. 1998. "New Frontiers in Diagnosing and Combating Corruption." *OECD Public Management Forum* IV(6).

Kaufmann, Daniel, and Shanag-Jin Wei. 1999. "Does 'Grease Money' Speed Up the Wheels of Commerce?" Policy Research Working Paper 2254 World Bank Policy Research Department. Washington, D.C.

Khan, Mohsin S., and Manmohan S. Kumar. 1993. "Public and Private Investment and the Convergence of per Capita Incomes in Developing Countries." IMF Working Paper 51. Washington, D.C.

————. 1997. "Public and Private Investment and The Growth Process in Developing Countries." *Oxford Bulletin of Economics and Statistics*, 59(1): 69-88.

Khan, Mohsin, and Carmen Reinhart. 1990. "Private Investment and Economic Growth in Developing Countries." *World Development* 18(1):19-27.

Knack, Stephen, and Philip Keefer. 1995. "Institutions and Economic Performance: Cross–Country Tests Using Alternative Institutional Measures." *Economics and Politics*,7(3):207-27.

Koyck, L. M. 1954. *Distributed Lags and Investment Analysis*. Amsterdam: North-Holland.

Larrain, F. and R. Vergara. 1993. "Investment and Macroeconomic Adjustment: The Case of East Asia." In L. Serven and A. Solimano, eds. *Striving for Growth after Adjustment: The Role of Capital Formation*. Washington, D.C: World Bank.

Leff, Nathaniel. 1989. "Economic Development Through Bureaucratic Corruption." *Political Corruption* 1964:389-403.

Looney, Robert E., and Peter C. Frederiken. 1997. "Government Investment and Follow-on Private Sector Investment in Pakistan, 1972-1995." *Journal of Economic Development* 22(1):91-100.

Mauro, Paolo. 1995. "Corruption and Growth." *Quarterly Journal of Economics* 110(August):681-712.

Monadjemi, Mehdi S., and Hyeonseung Huh. 1998. "Private and Government Investment: A Study of Three OECD Countries." *International Economic Journal*,12(2):93-105.

Moudud, Jamee K. 2000. "Crowding In or Crowding Out? A Classical-Harrodian Perspective." Working Paper 315. Bard College, Jerome Levy Economics Institute. New York.

Musalem, Alberto R. 1989. "Private Investment in Mexico: an Empirical Analysis." WPS 183, World Bank. Washington, D.C.

Nazmi, Nader, and Miguel D. Ramirez. 1997. "Public and Private Investment and Economic Growth in Mexico." *Contemporary Economic Policy*15(1):65-75.

Odedokun, M.O. 1997. "Relative Effects of Public Versus Private Investment Spending on Economic Efficiency and Growth in Developing Countries." *Applied Economics* 29(10):1325-36.

Ojo, O., and T. Oshikoya .1995. "Determinants of Long-term Growth: Some African Results." *Journal of African Economies* 4(2):163-91.

Oshikoya, Temitope W. 1994. "Macroeconomic Determinants of Domestic Private Investment in Africa: An Empirical Analysis." *Economic Development and Cultural Change* 42(3):573-96.

Ozler, Sule and Dani Rodrik. 1992. "External Shocks, Politics, and Private Investment: Some Theory and Empirical Evidence." NBER Working Paper W3960. Cambridge, MA.

Pereira, Alfredo M., and Rafael Flores de Frutos. 1999. "Public Capital and Private Sector Performance in the United States." *Journal of Urban Economics* 46(99):300-22.

Pereira, Alfredo M. 2000. "Is All Public Capital Created Equal?" *Review of Economics and Statistics*, 82(3):513-18.

———. 2001. "On the Effects of Public Investment on Private Investment: What Crowds in What?" *Public Finance Review* 29(1):3-25.

Pesaran, Hashem M. and Ron Smith. 1995. "Estimating Long-run Relationships from Dynamic Heterogeneous Panels." *Journal of Econometrics* 68(1):79-113.

Pfeffermann, Guy, Gregory V. Kisunko, and Mariusz A. Sumlinski. 1999. "Trends in Private Investment in Developing Countries: Statistics for 1970-97." IFC Discussion Paper 37, Washington, D.C.

Podrecca, Elena, and Gaetano Carmeci. 2001. "Fixed Investment and Economic Growth: New Results on Causality." *Applied Economics* 33(2):177-182.

Reinikka, Ritva and Jakob Svensson. 1999. "How Inadequate Provision of Public Infrastructure and Services Affects Private Investment." Policy Research Working Paper 2262, World Bank, Policy Research Department. Washington, D.C.

Rose-Ackerman, Susan. 1996. "Second-Generation Issues in Transition: Corruption." Annual World Bank Conference on Development Economics. 1995:373-78.

Sakr, Khaled. 1993. "Determinants of Private Investment in Pakistan." IMF Working Paper 30. Washington, D.C.

Savvides, A. "Economic Growth in Africa." 1995. *World Development* 23(3):449-58.

Serven, Luis, and Andres Solimano. 1990. "Private Investment and Macroeconomic Adjustment: Theory, Country Experience and Policy Implications." World Bank, Washington, D.C.

———. 1992. "Private Investment and Macroeconomic Adjustment: A Survey." *World Bank Research Observer* 7(1):95-114.

Shafik, Nemat. 1992. "Modeling Private Investment in Egypt." *Journal of Development Economics* 39 (2):263-77

Shleifer, Andrei and Robert W. Vishny. 1993. "Corruption." NBER Working Paper W4372. Cambridge, MA.

Sobhee, Sanjeev K. 1999. "Crowding-Out and the Effectiveness of Private Investment and Public Investment—The Case of Mauritius." *Indian Journal of Applied Economics* 8(3):143-62.

Solimano, Andres. 1989. "How Private Investment Reacts to Changing Macroeconomic Conditions: The Case of Chile." World Bank Working Paper 212. Washington, D.C.

Svensson, Jakob. 1998. "Investment, Property Rights, and Political Instability: Theory and Evidence." *European Economic Review* (42): 1317-1341.

Tanzi, Vito, and Hamid Davoodi. 1997. "Corruption, Public Investment, and Growth." IMF Working Paper WP/37/139. Washington, D.C.

———. 1998. "Corruption Around the World: Causes, Consequences, Scope, and Cures." IMF Working Paper WP/98/63. Washington, D.C.

———. 2000. "Corruption, Growth, and Public Finances." IMF Working Paper WP/00/182. Washington, D.C.

Theobald, Robin. 1990. *Corruption, Development and Underdevelopment*. Durham: Duke University Press.

Wade, Robert. 1982. "The System of Administrative and Political Corruption: Canal Irrigation in South India." *Journal of Development Studies*, 18(1): 287-328.

Wei, Shang-Jin. 1997. "How Taxing is Corruption on International Investors?" NBER Working Paper W6030. Cambridge, MA.

Wu, D. 1973. "Alternative Tests of Independence Between Stochastic Regressors and Disturbances." *Econometrica* 41(4):733-50.

Zebib, Mohammad, and Michael Muoghalu. 1998. "Dynamic Nature of Private Investment Function and Its Determinants in Developing Countries." *Studies in Economics and Finance* 18(2): 100-110.

Appendix A. Inter-Temporal Dynamics: Private Investment/GDP

The long-run consequences of investment decisions are of particular interest to policymakers and private investors. We can solve for long-run effects by adding a lagged dependent variable to the explanatory variables in our model via a Koyck transformation.[16] This allows for an investigation of the short- and long-run impact of independent variables. Assume that the long-run equilibrium level of our dependent variable is determined as in equation (1) below:

$$Y^* = a + bX_t, \qquad\qquad (1)$$

where
b is a vector of long-run effects.

Assume further that the adjustment process is described by equation (2) below. Investment levels change between periods but do not equilibrate in a single period, changing only by some proportion, *d,* of the gap between the previous period's output and the equilibrium level, Y^*:

$$Y_t - Y_{t-1} = (1-d)(Y_t^* - Y_{t-1}) + e_t \qquad (2)$$

where
d is the inter-temporal adjustment coefficient, and
e_t is the error term

Substituting (1) into (2) and collecting terms yields:

$$Y_t = (1-d)a + (1-d)bX_t + dY_{t-1} + e_t \qquad (3)$$

where

(1-d)b is the vector of short-run effects.

Then, using an estimate of the inter-temporal adjustment coefficient d, which is equal to a coefficient on the lagged dependent variable, and estimates of (1 - d)a and (1 - d)b, which are equal to the respective estimates of a constant and coefficients on independent variables, we solve for long run effects. Estimates of long run effects are reported in table A1 below.

---

[16] See Koyck (1954), Evans (1969).

TABLE A1. PRIVATE INVESTMENT DYNAMICS: LONG- AND SHORT-RUN EFFECTS

Independent variable		Full Sample	LAC	ASIA	SSAFR	ECA	MENA
Constant		1.704	2.680	4.451	3.944	3.953	2.989
Private investment/GDP lagged		0.886	0.807	0.886	0.098	0.865	0.694
Broad money/GDP	SR	0.020	0.023	0.022	0.165	-0.021	-0.002
	LR	0.178	0.122	0.192	0.183	-0.152	-0.007
External debt/GNP	SR	-0.006	-0.008	-0.034	-0.016	0.001	0.019
	LR	-0.055	-0.039	-0.297	-0.018	0.011	0.062
Current account balance/GDP	SR	-0.137	-0.183	-0.138	-0.061	0.089	-0.006
	LR	-1.203	-0.947	-1.215	-0.067	0.658	-0.020
(Public inv./GDP)*Corruption	SR	0.022	0.042	0.033	-0.190	0.022	0.018
	LR	0.191	0.217	0.286	-0.211	0.161	0.059
Public investment/GDP	SR	-0.160	-0.260	-0.323	0.695	-0.204	-0.069
	LR	-1.408	-1.346	-2.844	0.771	-1.505	-0.226

Fixed Investment Data

National accounts normally do not break down gross domestic investment into its private and public sector components. When they do, "private" investment often includes investment by state-owned enterprises such as state steel mills and so on. In this publication, we attempt to determine total public investment, inclusive of public investment undertaken by any state-owned enterprises. Private investment is then defined as the difference between total gross domestic investment (from national accounts) and consolidated public investment. Consolidated public investment data for each country were compiled mainly from World Bank Country Economic Memoranda, Public Investment Reviews, Public Expenditure Reviews, and other World Bank country reports. They reflect efforts by World Bank missions to compile public sector data. Where World Bank data were not available, country data were used.

The countries included in this edition represent all the developing countries for which the relevant data are available. Minor changes were made in the last two or three years for most countries because of revisions in their national accounts data. Updates are not available for Costa Rica, Mauritania, and Papua New Guinea.

Appendix C presents figures for each country in the sample displaying patterns of private fixed investment (PRIVATE I/GDP) and public fixed investment (Public I/GDP) from 1970 to 2000. The underlying data for these figures appears in table C.1, along with ratios on total fixed investment (GDFI/GDP). The ratios are computed using local currency units at current prices.

Appendix C. Country Charts

Sub-Saharan Africa

Benin

Comoros

Côte d'Ivoire

Guinea-Bissau

Kenya

Madagascar

Malawi

Mauritania

Mauritius

Namibia

Seychelles

South Africa

Benin

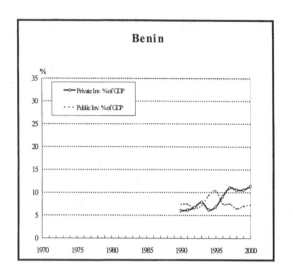

Guinea-Bissau

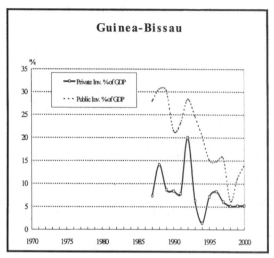

Comoros

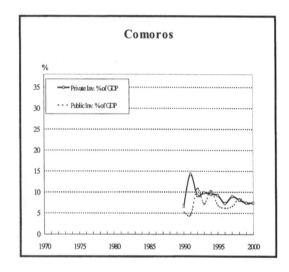

Kenya

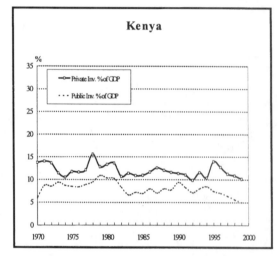

Côte d'Ivoire

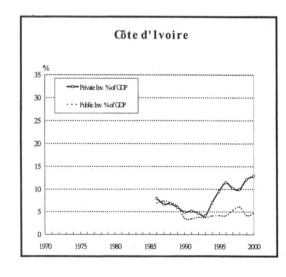

Madagascar

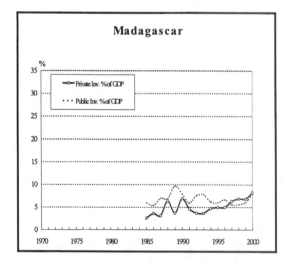

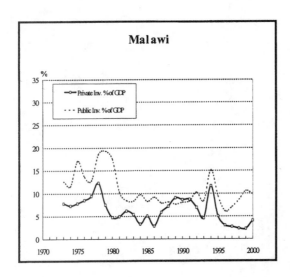

Malawi

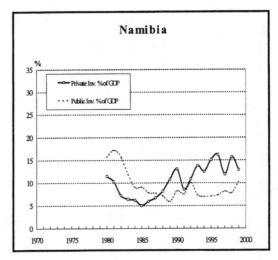

Namibia

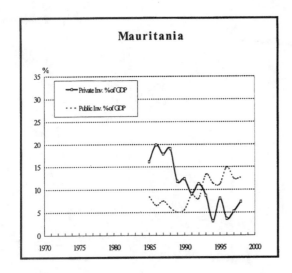

Mauritania

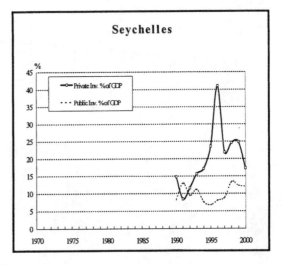

Seychelles

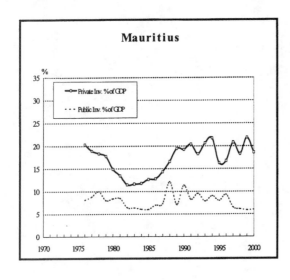

Mauritius

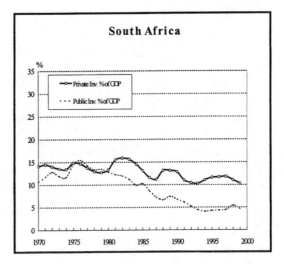

South Africa

Latin America and the Caribbean

Argentina

Barbados

Belize

Bolivia

Brazil

Chile

Colombia

Costa Rica

Dominica

Dominican Republic

Ecuador

El Salvador

Grenada

Guatemala

Guyana

Haiti

Mexico

Nicaragua

Panama

Paraguay

Peru

St. Lucia

St. Vincent

Trinidad & Tobago

Uruguay

Venezuela, Republica Bolivariana de

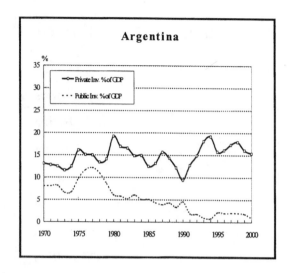

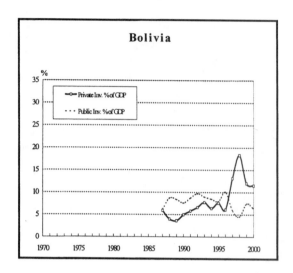

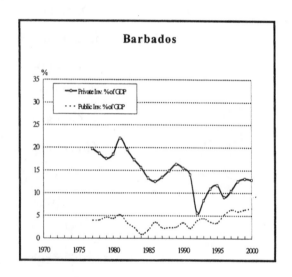

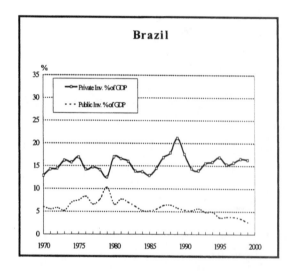

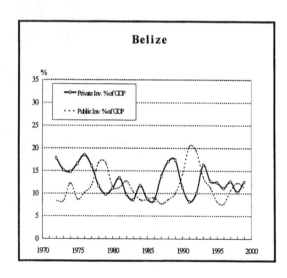

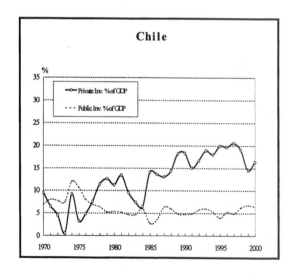

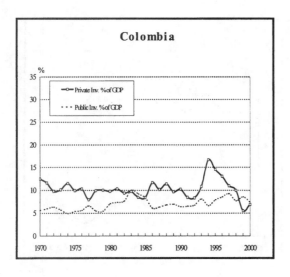

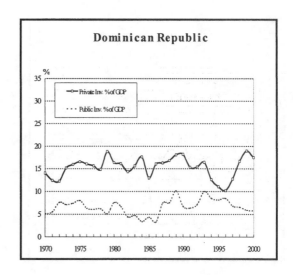

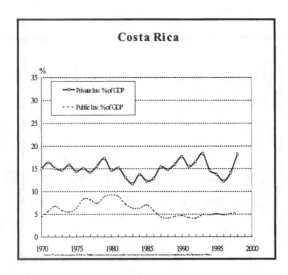

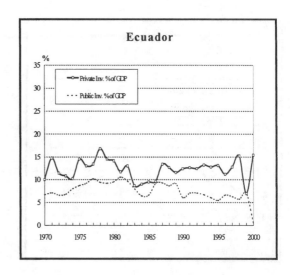

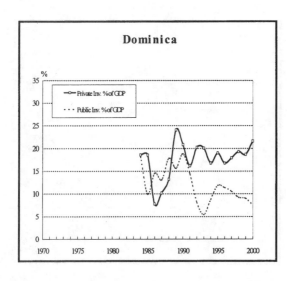

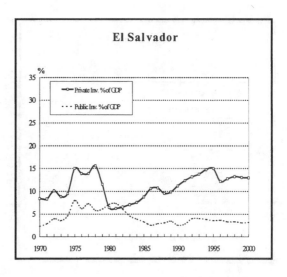

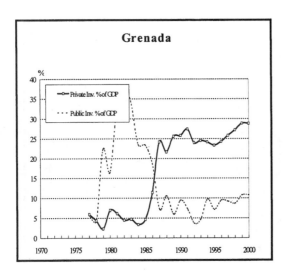

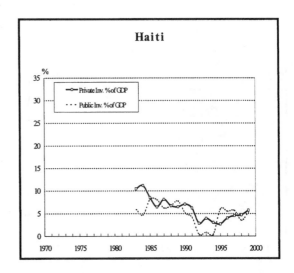

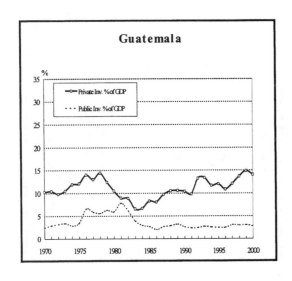

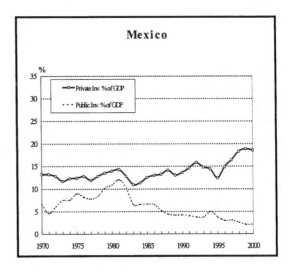

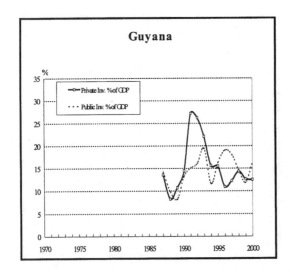

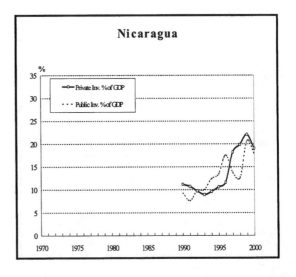

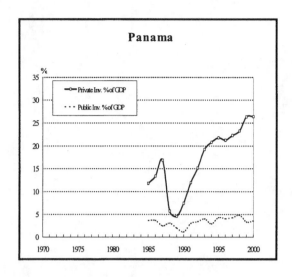

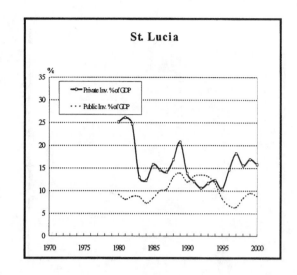

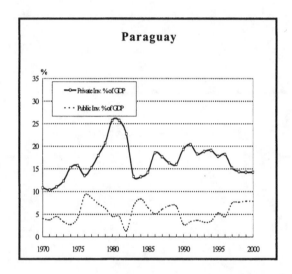

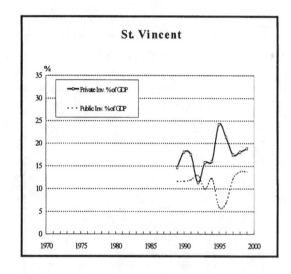

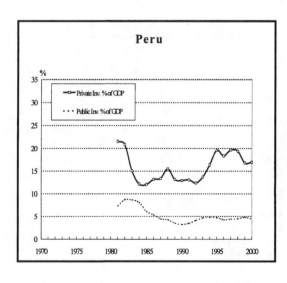

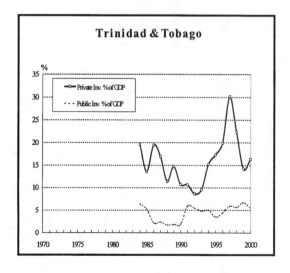

41

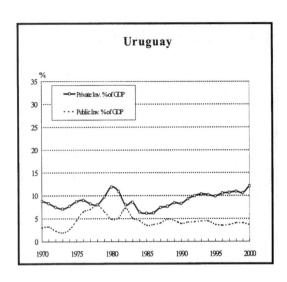

Uruguay

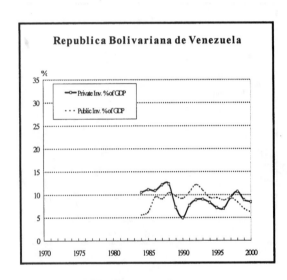

Republica Bolivariana de Venezuela

Middle East and North Africa

Egypt

Iran

Morocco

Tunisia

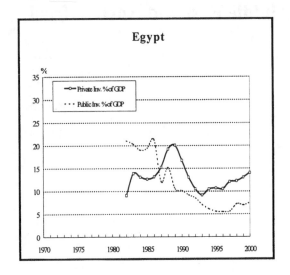

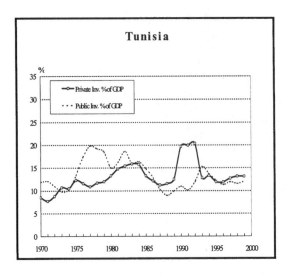

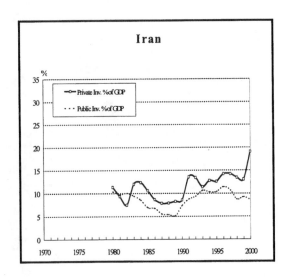

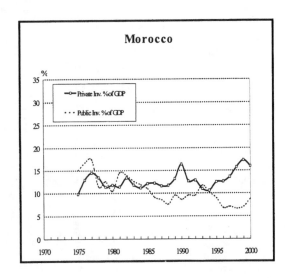

Europe and Central Asia

Azerbaijan

Bulgaria

Estonia

Kazakhstan

Lithuania

Poland

Romania

Turkey

Uzbekistan

Yugoslavia, Federal Republic of

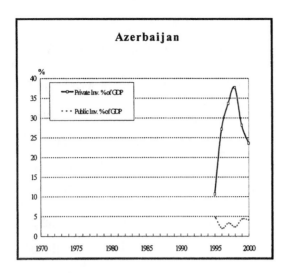

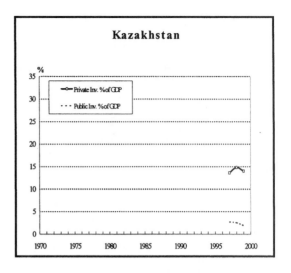

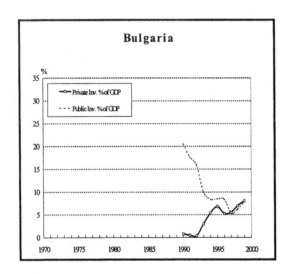

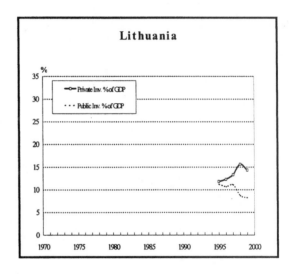

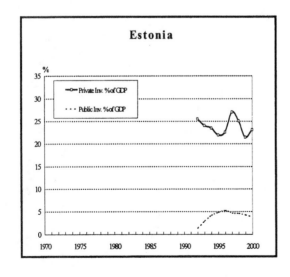

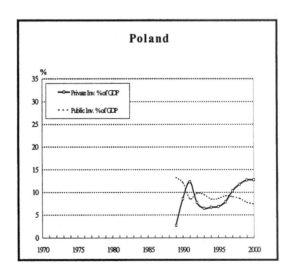

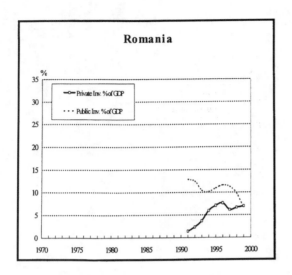

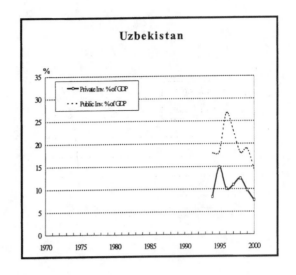

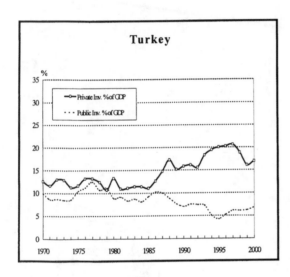

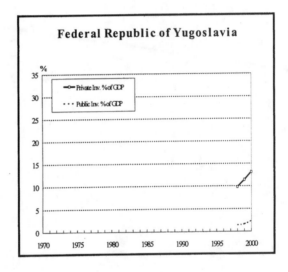

47

East Asia

Cambodia

China

Indonesia

Korea, Republic of

Malaysia

Papua New Guinea

Philippines

Thailand

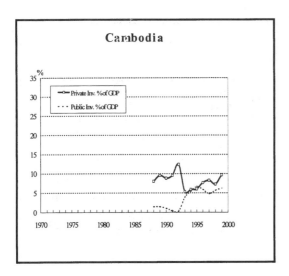

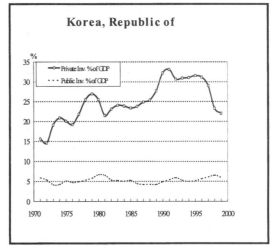

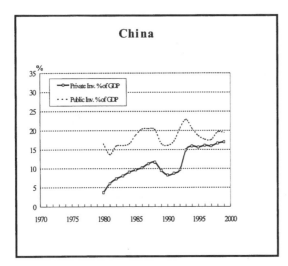

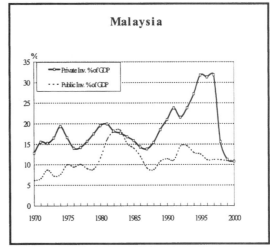

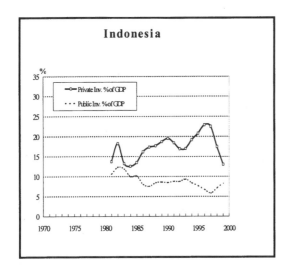

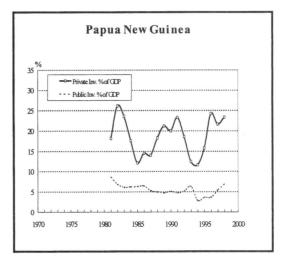

50

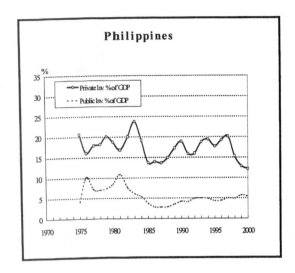

Philippines

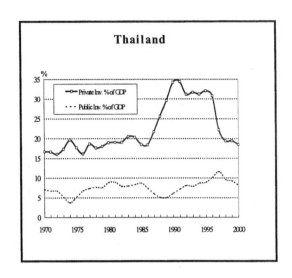

Thailand

South Asia

Bangladesh

India

Pakistan

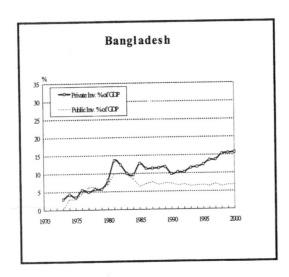

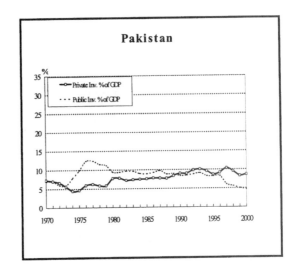

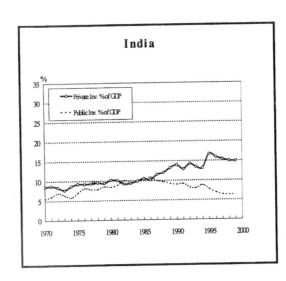

TABLE C1. INVESTMENT AS A SHARE OF GDP (IN %)

Country/Year		1970	1971	1972	1973	1974	1975	1976	1977	1978	1979	1980	1981	1982	1983	1984	1985	1986	1987	1988	1989	1990	1991	1992	1993	1994	1995	1996	1997	1998	1999	2000
Argentina	GDFI/GDP	21.2	20.9	20.7	18.2	19.3	25.9	26.8	27.2	24.4	22.7	25.3	22.7	21.8	20.9	20.0	17.6	17.5	19.6	18.6	15.5	14.0	14.6	16.7	19.1	19.9	17.9	18.1	19.4	19.9	17.9	16.3
	Private I/GDP	13.1	12.8	12.5	11.6	12.5	16.1	15.1	15.0	13.4	14.1	19.2	16.6	14.8	14.9	12.5	11.4	13.2	15.7	14.4	12.2	9.4	12.7	14.9	18.1	19.1	15.8	16.1	17.3	17.9	16.1	15.4
	Public I/GDP	8.1	8.1	8.2	6.6	6.8	9.8	11.7	12.2	11.0	8.6	6.1	5.8	5.2	6.1	5.0	5.1	4.3	3.9	4.3	3.3	4.6	1.9	1.8	1.0	0.8	2.2	2.0	2.0	2.0	1.8	1.0
Azerbaijan	GDFI/GDP																										15.6	29.1	37.0	40.0	32.5	27.6
	Private I/GDP																										10.7	27.1	33.6	37.7	28.2	23.6
	Public I/GDP																										5.0	2.0	3.3	2.3	4.3	4.1
Bangladesh	GDFI/GDP				3.0	7.1	6.3	9.9	11.1	11.8	11.3	15.3	23.5	22.6	19.7	18.1	19.1	18.5	19.0	18.4	19.1	17.1	16.9	17.3	17.9	18.4	19.1	20.0	20.7	21.6	22.2	22.4
	Private I/GDP				2.9	4.2	3.4	5.4	4.9	5.6	5.7	8.2	13.6	12.4	10.0	9.6	12.7	11.4	11.4	11.5	11.7	9.8	10.3	10.3	11.5	11.8	12.4	13.6	13.7	15.3	15.5	15.7
	Public I/GDP				0.1	2.9	2.9	4.6	6.2	6.2	5.6	7.1	9.9	10.2	9.8	8.4	6.4	7.2	7.7	6.9	7.3	7.2	6.6	7.0	6.5	6.6	6.7	6.4	7.0	6.4	6.7	6.7
Barbados	GDFI/GDP								23.7	22.7	22.2	22.8	27.2	22.8	19.6	16.5	15.1	16.1	15.8	17.3	18.8	18.9	16.2	9.5	12.7	14.5	15.1	14.2	16.7	18.5	19.4	19.5
	Private I/GDP								19.7	18.7	17.5	18.5	22.0	19.5	17.3	15.6	13.3	12.6	13.5	14.9	16.3	15.5	14.0	5.6	8.3	10.9	11.7	9.1	10.4	12.6	13.1	12.9
	Public I/GDP								4.0	4.0	4.6	4.3	5.2	3.3	2.4	0.9	1.8	3.6	2.3	2.4	2.5	3.5	2.2	3.9	4.4	3.6	3.4	5.2	6.3	5.9	6.3	6.6
Belize	GDFI/GDP			26.2	23.5	27.1	25.3	28.7	28.0	28.5	26.6	22.7	24.8	22.5	18.9	20.3	17.4	17.4	21.5	25.7	27.4	25.6	28.5	29.3	29.8	24.1	20.6	18.8	23.3	22.6	23.8	
	Private I/GDP			17.8	15.2	14.8	16.6	18.5	16.1	11.7	9.8	11.1	13.5	9.8	8.5	11.8	8.7	8.4	13.8	15.7	18.8	15.4	8.1	10.0	16.3	12.8	12.4	11.1	12.7	10.3	12.5	
	Public I/GDP			8.4	8.3	12.3	8.7	10.2	11.9	16.8	16.8	11.5	11.3	12.7	10.4	8.6	8.7	9.0	7.7	10.0	8.6	10.2	20.4	19.3	13.5	11.3	8.2	7.7	10.6	12.3	11.3	
Benin	GDFI/GDP																		12.1	12.7	12.0	13.4	13.6	13.2	15.0	14.9	15.5	16.2	16.6	18.5	17.6	18.6
	Private I/GDP																		5.9	4.0	3.6	6.0	6.1	6.7	7.9	6.2	6.9	9.1	11.0	10.5	10.6	11.3
	Public I/GDP																		6.2	8.7	8.4	7.4	7.5	6.5	7.1	8.7	8.6	7.1	5.6	8.0	7.0	7.3
Bolivia	GDFI/GDP																					12.6	14.5	16.3	16.7	14.9	15.5	16.2	19.0	22.8	19.4	17.9
	Private I/GDP																					5.0	5.8	6.6	7.7	6.4	7.6	6.1	13.1	18.3	12.0	11.5
	Public I/GDP																					7.6	8.7	9.7	9.0	8.5	8.0	10.1	5.9	4.5	7.5	6.4
Brazil	GDFI/GDP	18.8	19.7	20.2	21.4	22.8	24.4	22.5	21.3	21.8	22.8	23.6	24.3	23.0	19.9	18.9	18.0	20.0	23.2	24.3	26.9	22.9	19.6	19.6	20.4	20.7	20.5	19.1	19.5	19.9	18.9	
	Private I/GDP	12.8	14.2	14.4	16.2	15.8	16.9	14.2	14.7	14.1	12.5	17.0	16.6	16.0	13.8	13.7	12.9	14.4	16.8	17.9	21.1	17.6	14.4	13.9	15.5	15.8	16.8	15.3	15.7	16.5	16.3	
	Public I/GDP	6.0	5.5	5.8	5.2	7.0	7.5	8.3	6.6	7.7	10.3	6.6	7.7	7.0	6.1	5.2	5.1	5.6	6.4	6.4	5.8	5.3	5.2	5.7	4.9	4.9	3.7	3.9	3.8	3.4	2.6	
Bulgaria	GDFI/GDP																					21.3	18.2	16.2	13.0	13.8	15.3	13.6	10.8	13.2	15.9	
	Private I/GDP																					0.8	0.5	0.3	2.9	5.4	6.8	5.3	5.5	7.0	8.0	
	Public I/GDP																					20.5	17.7	15.9	10.0	8.4	8.5	8.4	5.3	6.2	7.9	
Cambodia	GDFI/GDP																			9.4	11.0	9.8	9.9	12.7	9.2	11.3	12.7	13.5	13.0	12.9	15.8	
	Private I/GDP																			8.0	9.5	8.8	9.5	12.4	5.3	5.9	6.0	7.6	8.2	7.3	9.6	
	Public I/GDP																			1.4	1.5	1.0	0.3	0.3	3.9	5.4	6.7	5.9	4.8	5.7	6.2	
Chile	GDFI/GDP	16.4	14.5	12.2	7.9	21.2	13.9	12.8	14.5	17.8	17.8	16.6	18.6	14.2	12.0	12.4	16.8	17.1	19.4	20.3	23.0	23.1	19.9	22.4	24.9	23.3	23.9	24.9	25.5	25.2	21.3	22.8
	Private I/GDP	9.5	6.5	4.5	0.5	9.2	3.2	4.8	7.6	11.4	12.6	11.2	13.4	9.5	7.4	6.4	14.1	13.6	13.1	14.4	18.2	18.4	15.0	16.7	18.9	18.0	19.9	19.7	20.6	19.0	14.5	16.4
	Public I/GDP	6.9	8.0	7.7	7.4	12.0	10.7	8.0	6.9	6.4	5.2	5.4	5.2	4.7	4.7	6.0	2.8	3.5	6.4	5.9	4.8	4.8	4.9	5.8	6.0	5.3	3.9	5.2	4.9	6.3	6.8	6.4
China	GDFI/GDP											20.2	19.8	23.2	24.1	25.6	28.4	30.6	31.7	31.8	26.1	24.4	25.9	30.3	37.7	36.4	34.2	33.8	33.5	36.3	36.4	
	Private I/GDP											3.7	6.0	7.3	8.1	9.0	9.6	10.2	11.2	11.6	9.5	8.3	8.7	9.7	14.9	15.9	15.6	16.1	15.9	16.6	17.0	
	Public I/GDP											16.5	13.7	16.0	16.0	16.5	18.7	20.4	20.5	20.2	16.6	16.1	17.2	20.6	22.9	20.6	18.6	17.7	17.6	19.6	19.5	

Continued

TABLE C1. INVESTMENT AS A SHARE OF GDP (IN %) (Continued)

Country/Year		1970	1971	1972	1973	1974	1975	1976	1977	1978	1979	1980	1981	1982	1983	1984	1985	1986	1987	1988	1989	1990	1991	1992	1993	1994	1995	1996	1997	1998	1999	2000
Colombia	GDFI/GDP	18.0	17.5	16.1	15.8	16.4	15.3	15.9	14.5	15.4	15.4	16.8	17.7	17.0	19.7	17.7	16.7	17.7	16.5	18.2	16.6	16.6	15.0	15.1	18.9	23.3	22.4	21.5	20.2	17.6	14.1	14.3
	Private I/GDP	12.4	11.6	9.8	10.1	11.5	9.9	10.3	7.9	9.9	10.0	9.8	10.3	9.4	9.7	8.5	8.4	11.6	10.2	11.4	9.6	10.2	8.4	8.3	10.8	16.7	14.5	13.0	11.0	9.9	5.5	6.9
	Public I/GDP	5.6	6.0	6.3	5.7	4.9	5.4	5.6	6.6	5.5	5.4	7.0	7.4	7.6	10.0	9.2	8.3	6.1	6.3	6.8	7.0	6.4	6.5	6.7	8.1	6.6	7.9	8.5	9.2	7.7	8.6	7.4
Comoros	GDFI/GDP																					11.9	18.9	20.1	17.0	19.8	16.1	13.5	15.5	16.6	14.6	15.0
	Private I/GDP																					6.7	14.3	9.2	9.8	9.5	9.2	7.3	8.9	8.1	7.4	7.4
	Public I/GDP																					5.2	4.6	10.9	7.2	10.4	6.9	6.2	6.6	8.5	7.2	7.6
Costa Rica	GDFI/GDP	19.4	22.1	20.5	20.5	21.3	20.7	23.5	22.4	23.0	26.2	23.9	24.1	20.3	18.0	20.0	19.3	18.7	19.8	18.9	20.5	22.4	19.7	20.8	23.2	19.5	18.9	17.1	19.2	23.7		
	Private I/GDP	15.0	16.4	15.1	14.7	15.8	14.4	15.1	14.2	15.6	17.3	14.7	15.2	13.1	11.6	13.7	12.3	12.9	15.4	14.8	16.0	17.7	15.5	16.6	18.3	14.6	13.8	12.2	14.0	18.2		
	Public I/GDP	4.4	5.7	5.4	5.8	5.5	6.3	8.4	8.2	7.4	8.9	9.2	8.9	7.2	6.4	6.4	7.0	5.8	4.4	4.1	4.5	4.7	4.2	4.1	4.9	4.8	5.1	4.8	5.1	5.5		
Cote d'Ivoire	GDFI/GDP																	14.8	14.1	13.8	12.2	8.5	8.6	8.5	7.8	11.1	13.6	15.6	15.5	16.0	16.3	17.6
	Private I/GDP																	7.9	6.7	6.8	5.9	4.9	5.1	4.7	4.1	7.0	9.5	11.4	10.2	9.9	12.1	12.9
	Public I/GDP																	6.9	7.4	7.0	6.3	3.6	3.4	3.8	3.7	4.1	4.2	4.2	5.3	6.1	4.2	4.7
Dominica	GDFI/GDP															36.8	28.5	22.3	23.3	31.1	39.6	39.7	30.5	28.4	25.5	25.5	30.8	28.1	28.5	28.5	27.7	29.1
	Private I/GDP															18.6	18.6	7.8	10.2	13.2	24.0	20.8	16.2	20.2	20.1	16.8	19.0	16.7	17.9	19.3	18.7	21.6
	Public I/GDP															18.2	9.9	14.5	13.1	17.9	15.6	18.9	14.4	8.1	5.4	8.8	11.8	11.4	10.5	9.2	9.0	7.5
Dominican Rep.	GDFI/GDP	19.1	17.9	19.8	22.2	23.3	24.5	22.3	21.7	21.0	23.9	23.9	22.8	18.7	20.3	21.0	17.3	19.3	23.7	24.3	28.2	24.9	21.6	22.5	26.4	21.1	19.2	18.7	19.5	23.1	24.8	23.2
	Private I/GDP	14.0	12.4	12.2	15.1	15.9	16.5	16.0	15.6	14.8	18.8	16.3	16.1	14.3	15.6	17.6	12.9	16.0	16.2	18.1	18.2	15.3	16.4	15.4	16.4	12.6	11.0	10.2	12.7	16.6	18.9	17.5
	Public I/GDP	5.1	5.5	7.6	7.1	7.4	8.0	6.3	6.1	6.2	5.1	7.6	6.7	4.4	4.7	3.4	4.4	3.3	7.5	6.2	10.0	9.6	5.2	7.1	10.0	8.5	8.2	8.5	6.8	6.5	5.9	5.8
Ecuador	GDFI/GDP	16.7	21.8	18.0	17.6	18.2	23.2	22.2	23.6	26.2	23.7	23.6	22.3	22.7	16.6	15.4	16.1	18.8	22.7	21.3	20.7	18.4	19.7	19.5	19.9	18.8	18.6	17.8	19.0	21.0	14.0	15.9
	Private I/GDP	10.0	14.7	11.4	10.8	10.2	14.5	13.0	13.4	16.8	14.5	14.1	11.7	13.0	8.6	9.0	9.5	9.6	13.4	12.7	11.6	12.4	12.6	12.4	13.2	12.8	13.1	11.2	12.8	15.2	6.9	15.4
	Public I/GDP	6.7	7.1	6.6	6.8	8.0	8.7	9.2	10.2	9.4	9.2	9.5	10.6	9.7	8.0	6.4	6.6	9.2	9.3	8.6	9.2	6.1	7.0	7.1	6.7	6.0	5.5	6.6	6.3	5.7	7.1	0.5
Egypt	GDFI/GDP													30.1	34.2	32.1	32.1	34.4	27.3	34.4	30.6	26.9	22.2	19.1	16.2	16.6	16.2	16.0	17.6	19.5	20.0	21.5
	Private I/GDP													9.1	13.9	13.1	12.7	13.1	14.2	19.2	20.1	16.7	13.0	10.6	9.1	10.5	10.7	10.4	12.0	12.3	13.0	14.0
	Public I/GDP													21.0	20.3	19.0	19.4	21.3	13.1	15.2	10.5	10.2	9.2	8.5	7.1	6.1	5.5	5.6	5.6	7.2	7.0	7.5
El Salvador	GDFI/GDP	10.7	11.2	14.1	12.4	14.2	23.0	20.1	21.2	21.4	17.6	13.6	13.6	12.6	11.6	11.5	12.0	13.1	13.6	12.6	13.3	13.7	15.2	17.2	17.8	18.6	18.6	15.8	16.1	16.6	16.2	16.2
	Private I/GDP	8.4	8.3	10.1	8.8	9.5	15.0	13.9	13.9	15.6	11.5	6.4	6.2	6.5	7.0	7.6	8.7	10.6	10.7	9.5	9.8	11.2	12.3	13.2	13.7	14.7	15.0	12.1	12.7	13.2	13.0	13.0
	Public I/GDP	2.3	2.9	4.0	3.6	4.7	8.0	6.2	7.3	5.8	6.1	7.1	7.3	6.1	4.6	3.9	3.3	2.5	2.9	3.1	3.5	2.5	2.8	4.0	4.0	3.8	3.6	3.7	3.3	3.3	3.1	3.2
Estonia	GDFI/GDP																							26.9	26.9	27.6	26.7	27.8	31.7	29.7	25.7	26.9
	Private I/GDP																							25.5	24.0	23.5	21.9	22.6	27.0	25.1	21.4	23.1
	Public I/GDP																							1.3	2.9	4.2	4.8	5.2	4.7	4.6	4.2	3.8
Grenada	GDFI/GDP								11.5	8.6	24.6	23.3	38.4	41.7	39.1	26.9	28.0	30.1	31.4	32.2	31.5	35.3	34.7	27.7	29.2	33.9	30.5	33.7	35.0	35.9	39.6	39.6
	Private I/GDP								5.9	4.3	2.3	6.9	6.1	4.5	4.7	3.4	4.6	11.4	24.2	21.6	25.6	25.8	27.4	24.0	24.5	24.1	23.3	24.3	25.8	27.2	28.8	28.8
	Public I/GDP								5.6	4.3	22.4	16.4	32.3	37.2	34.4	23.5	23.4	18.7	7.2	10.6	5.9	9.5	7.3	3.7	4.7	9.8	7.1	9.5	9.2	8.7	10.8	10.8
Guatemala	GDFI/GDP	12.6	13.3	13.0	13.9	14.8	15.6	20.6	18.9	20.0	18.7	16.4	16.8	15.0	10.5	9.6	11.0	10.1	12.4	13.4	13.7	13.0	12.2	15.6	16.1	14.2	14.5	13.3	15.1	16.6	17.9	16.8
	Private I/GDP	10.2	10.4	9.8	10.5	11.9	12.1	14.0	13.0	14.4	12.4	10.5	8.9	8.9	6.6	6.7	8.3	8.1	9.7	10.5	10.6	10.4	9.8	13.2	13.4	11.7	12.0	10.8	12.1	13.7	14.8	14.0
	Public I/GDP	2.4	2.9	3.2	3.4	2.9	3.5	6.6	5.9	5.6	6.3	5.9	7.8	6.1	3.9	2.9	2.7	2.0	2.7	2.9	3.2	2.6	2.4	2.4	2.7	2.6	2.5	2.5	3.1	3.0	3.1	2.8

Continued

Country/Year		1970	1971	1972	1973	1974	1975	1976	1977	1978	1979	1980	1981	1982	1983	1984	1985	1986	1987	1988	1989	1990	1991	1992	1993	1994	1995	1996	1997	1998	1999	2000
Guinea-Bissau	GDFI/GDP																		35.2	44.7	39.0	29.9	31.0	48.4	30.9	21.8	22.3	23.0	21.6	11.3	16.3	19.2
	Private I/GDP																		7.3	14.1	8.7	8.4	7.8	20.0	6.3	1.4	7.1	8.3	6.1	5.2	5.2	5.3
	Public I/GDP																		27.9	30.6	30.3	21.5	23.2	28.4	24.6	20.4	15.2	14.8	15.6	6.2	11.1	13.9
Guyana	GDFI/GDP																		27.8	18.0	18.9	27.7	42.2	42.3	41.5	27.2	31.7	30.0	30.3	28.8	24.5	28.7
	Private I/GDP																		13.6	8.2	10.7	14.4	27.2	26.2	22.1	15.6	15.5	10.9	12.3	14.3	12.6	12.5
	Public I/GDP																		14.2	9.8	8.2	13.3	15.1	16.1	19.4	11.6	16.3	19.1	18.1	14.5	11.8	16.2
Haiti	GDFI/GDP															16.3	15.9	16.7	14.5	14.3	13.4	14.3	12.2	10.3	3.2	4.8	3.4	8.7	9.5	10.2	8.2	11.0
	Private I/GDP															10.4	11.2	8.5	6.4	8.1	6.7	6.5	7.8	6.2	2.9	3.9	3.0	2.7	4.0	4.5	4.7	5.7
	Public I/GDP															5.9	4.7	8.1	8.0	6.2	6.7	7.8	5.1	4.2	0.3	0.9	0.4	6.0	5.5	5.7	3.5	5.3
India	GDFI/GDP	14.0	14.7	15.3	14.0	14.4	16.2	17.3	17.2	17.4	17.9	18.5	18.9	18.8	19.6	20.6	21.1	21.4	21.6	22.4	22.9	22.0	22.4	21.4	21.9	24.4	22.8	21.7	21.2	21.2	21.2	
	Private I/GDP	8.5	8.7	8.3	7.7	8.6	9.2	9.2	9.3	9.5	9.3	10.1	10.1	9.1	9.3	10.5	10.2	11.5	12.0	13.2	13.9	12.9	14.2	13.4	13.2	15.9	16.7	15.4	15.0	14.9		
	Public I/GDP	5.5	6.0	7.0	6.3	5.8	7.0	8.1	7.8	7.9	8.5	8.4	8.9	10.1	9.5	10.1	10.9	10.0	9.6	9.2	9.0	9.2	8.2	8.0	8.8	7.7	6.9	6.4	6.3	6.4		
Indonesia	GDFI/GDP												24.2	30.5	25.1	22.5	23.6	24.2	24.9	26.1	27.3	28.0	27.2	25.6	26.3	27.6	28.4	29.6	28.3	24.6	21.2	
	Private I/GDP												13.7	18.2	13.2	12.5	13.5	16.2	17.3	17.7	18.7	19.5	18.4	16.9	17.0	19.2	20.8	22.9	22.5	17.4	12.9	
	Public I/GDP												10.5	12.3	11.9	9.9	10.1	8.0	7.5	8.4	8.6	8.5	8.8	8.7	9.3	8.4	7.7	6.7	5.8	7.1	8.3	
Iran	GDFI/GDP											21.7	19.1	17.5	21.5	20.9	17.5	15.4	13.3	13.3	13.3	15.8	22.3	22.7	22.1	23.1	23.0	25.7	24.9	22.1	22.2	27.6
	Private I/GDP											11.4	9.3	7.4	12.0	12.4	10.6	8.6	7.8	7.9	8.2	8.5	13.6	13.4	11.4	12.8	12.6	14.2	14.2	13.4	13.0	19.0
	Public I/GDP											10.4	9.8	10.0	9.4	8.5	6.9	6.7	5.5	5.4	7.3	7.3	8.7	9.3	10.7	10.3	10.4	11.5	10.7	8.7	9.2	8.6
Kazakhstan	GDFI/GDP																													16.3	17.3	15.9
	Private I/GDP																													13.6	14.8	14.0
	Public I/GDP																													2.7	2.5	1.9
Kenya	GDFI/GDP	19.7	22.7	20.8	19.2	20.2	20.0	21.0	25.1	23.9	23.7	23.6	18.0	19.0	18.1	17.9	19.6	19.6	20.1	19.3	20.7	19.3	17.0	19.6	18.9	21.4	19.8	17.6	16.5	15.1		
	Private I/GDP	13.7	14.0	13.6	11.4	11.7	11.6	12.1	15.6	13.6	12.8	13.3	11.4	10.7	10.9	10.9	11.6	12.6	12.0	11.6	11.3	11.0	9.8	11.5	10.4	13.9	12.7	11.2	10.8	10.1		
	Public I/GDP	6.0	8.7	9.4	8.5	8.7	8.4	8.9	9.5	10.3	10.9	10.2	6.7	8.4	7.2	7.0	8.0	7.1	8.0	7.8	9.4	8.3	7.1	8.0	8.5	7.4	7.0	6.4	5.6	5.0		
Korea, Rep. of	GDFI/GDP	21.5	19.9	23.2	25.1	25.2	23.9	26.7	30.7	32.7	32.1	28.0	28.4	29.2	28.9	28.6	29.1	29.6	31.9	37.1	38.4	36.6	36.2	36.0	36.7	36.8	35.1	29.8	28.0			
	Private I/GDP	15.6	14.6	19.1	20.8	20.1	19.2	21.8	25.4	26.9	25.5	21.4	23.0	24.0	23.8	23.3	24.8	25.3	27.7	32.2	33.1	30.7	30.9	31.0	31.5	31.1	29.0	23.2	22.0			
	Public I/GDP	5.9	5.3	4.2	4.2	5.1	4.7	4.9	5.3	5.8	6.7	6.5	5.3	5.2	4.2	5.2	4.4	4.3	4.9	5.4	5.3	5.9	5.0	5.2	5.7	6.1	6.1	6.5	6.0			
Lithuania	GDFI/GDP																											23.0	23.0	24.4	24.3	22.5
	Private I/GDP																											11.8	12.3	13.3	15.6	14.3
	Public I/GDP																											11.2	10.7	11.1	8.7	8.2
Madagascar	GDFI/GDP																8.5	9.0	10.1	13.3	13.4	14.8	10.6	11.3	11.4	10.9	11.6	11.9	12.5	12.9	16.1	
	Private I/GDP																2.6	3.6	3.1	6.4	6.9	6.9	4.6	3.7	3.7	4.7	5.0	6.3	6.9	6.8	8.2	
	Public I/GDP																6.0	5.4	7.0	6.9	7.9	7.9	6.0	7.6	7.7	6.2	6.7	5.6	6.1	6.1	7.9	
Malawi	GDFI/GDP	20.4	18.9	24.9	22.1	22.2	30.9	26.8	22.2	15.1	14.6	13.7	13.0	13.3	13.8	15.3	16.7	16.7	14.8	17.0	17.2					13.0	11.4	9.1	9.8	11.0	12.8	13.9
	Private I/GDP	7.8	7.3	7.8	8.5	9.4	7.5	4.7	12.3	4.9	5.4	6.1	5.4	5.9	5.9	7.2	8.6	9.0	8.6	8.7	6.9					4.6	3.0	2.8	3.0	2.3	2.2	4.1
	Public I/GDP	12.6	11.6	17.1	13.6	12.8	19.3	17.5	18.6	10.2	8.4	8.3	8.0	7.9	7.9	8.0	8.0	8.6	6.9	8.3	10.2					8.4	8.4	6.1	7.1	8.6	10.6	9.8

Continued

TABLE C1. INVESTMENT AS A SHARE OF GDP (IN %) (Continued)

Country/Year		1970	1971	1972	1973	1974	1975	1976	1977	1978	1979	1980	1981	1982	1983	1984	1985	1986	1987	1988	1989	1990	1991	1992	1993	1994	1995	1996	1997	1998	1999	2000
Malaysia	GDFI/GDP	18.9	22.1	23.9	23.7	26.9	26.6	23.4	24.3	24.7	26.4	31.1	36.0	36.3	36.0	31.9	29.8	26.3	23.0	24.1	29.3	32.4	34.9	36.0	38.3	40.1	44.3	42.5	43.1	26.8	22.3	21.9
	Private I/GDP	12.8	15.5	15.2	16.5	19.3	16.6	14.0	14.2	15.7	17.5	19.5	19.9	18.2	17.7	16.8	15.8	14.3	13.8	15.4	18.5	20.9	23.7	21.5	23.8	27.2	31.7	31.3	31.8	15.6	11.3	10.8
	Public I/GDP	6.1	6.6	8.7	7.2	7.6	10.0	9.4	10.1	9.0	8.9	11.6	16.1	18.2	18.4	15.1	14.0	12.1	9.1	8.7	10.8	11.5	11.1	14.5	14.6	13.0	12.6	11.2	11.3	11.2	11.0	11.1
Mauritania	GDFI/GDP																24.5	26.4	25.3	25.1	16.8	17.9	17.9	19.3	22.0	14.5	19.3	18.6	17.7	20.0		
	Private I/GDP																16.1	19.9	17.8	19.0	11.8	12.4	9.1	11.2	8.7	3.1	8.1	3.6	5.2	7.3		
	Public I/GDP																8.4	6.5	7.5	6.1	5.1	5.6	8.8	8.1	13.3	11.4	11.2	15.0	12.4	12.7		
Mauritius	GDFI/GDP							28.4	27.7	28.3	25.7	23.3	21.9	17.9	18.0	17.8	18.7	19.7	21.6	28.7	26.5	30.6	28.6	27.8	28.5	30.8	24.2	26.1	27.3	24.4	27.7	24.6
	Private I/GDP							20.3	18.9	18.3	17.7	14.9	13.5	11.5	11.6	11.8	12.6	12.8	14.3	16.6	19.5	19.2	20.4	18.3	20.6	21.7	16.3	16.7	20.8	18.3	21.8	18.6
	Public I/GDP							8.1	8.8	10.0	8.0	8.4	8.5	6.4	6.4	6.1	6.0	7.0	7.3	12.2	7.1	11.4	8.2	9.6	7.9	9.1	8.0	9.3	6.5	6.1	5.9	6.0
Mexico	GDFI/GDP	19.8	17.8	18.9	19.2	19.9	21.4	21.0	19.7	21.2	23.7	24.8	26.3	23.0	17.5	18.0	19.2	19.6	18.5	18.5	17.2	17.9	18.7	19.6	18.6	19.4	16.2	17.9	19.5	20.9	21.0	20.8
	Private I/GDP	13.2	13.2	12.8	11.7	12.3	12.4	12.8	11.9	12.8	13.5	13.9	14.3	12.8	11.0	11.4	12.5	13.0	13.3	14.1	13.0	13.6	14.6	15.8	14.8	14.3	12.4	14.9	16.4	18.3	18.9	18.6
	Public I/GDP	6.6	4.6	6.1	7.5	7.6	9.0	8.2	7.8	8.4	10.2	10.9	12.1	10.2	6.6	6.6	6.7	6.6	5.2	4.4	4.2	4.3	4.1	3.8	3.8	5.0	3.7	3.0	3.1	2.6	2.1	2.2
Morocco	GDFI/GDP						24.8	29.7	32.0	24.9	24.0	22.2	26.0	27.3	24.4	23.1	23.1	21.3	20.2	19.3	22.8	25.0	22.2	22.4	22.8	20.7	21.4	19.4	20.7	22.4	24.3	24.8
	Private I/GDP						9.8	12.9	14.5	13.5	11.4	11.8	11.4	13.4	11.8	11.2	12.1	12.2	11.6	11.8	13.2	16.4	12.7	12.8	11.0	10.6	12.5	12.6	13.6	15.7	17.3	16.0
	Public I/GDP						15.0	16.7	17.5	11.4	12.6	10.4	14.5	12.6	12.6	11.9	11.0	9.6	8.6	7.6	9.6	8.6	9.5	9.6	11.8	10.1	8.9	6.8	7.1	6.6	7.0	8.8
Namibia	GDFI/GDP											27.2	27.5	23.0	18.3	15.2	14.1	13.8	14.5	15.3	16.7	21.3	16.2	21.0	21.1	19.5	22.2	23.5	20.1	23.5	23.2	
	Private I/GDP											11.4	10.2	7.2	6.4	6.2	5.0	5.9	6.7	8.2	10.8	13.1	8.6	10.9	13.8	12.5	15.1	16.2	11.9	15.7	12.9	
	Public I/GDP											15.7	17.2	15.8	11.9	9.0	9.1	7.8	7.8	7.1	5.9	8.2	7.6	10.1	7.3	7.0	7.1	7.3	8.2	7.8	10.4	
Nicaragua	GDFI/GDP																					20.4	18.3	19.5	18.9	22.0	24.0	29.2	31.9	32.4	42.7	36.8
	Private I/GDP																					11.2	10.7	9.7	8.9	9.6	10.6	11.6	18.2	19.8	22.0	19.0
	Public I/GDP																					9.3	7.6	9.8	10.0	12.4	13.4	17.6	13.7	12.6	20.7	17.8
Pakistan	GDFI/GDP	14.3	14.0	12.6	11.5	12.2	14.4	18.2	18.6	17.3	17.0	17.1	17.1	16.8	17.0	16.5	16.5	17.0	17.5	16.5	17.3	17.3	17.4	18.6	19.1	17.9	16.9	17.4	16.4	15.1	13.3	13.3
	Private I/GDP	7.3	7.0	6.6	5.6	4.4	4.6	5.9	6.2	5.8	5.8	7.7	7.8	7.2	7.4	7.5	7.6	7.8	7.7	7.7	8.3	8.9	8.9	9.8	10.0	9.6	8.7	9.1	10.3	9.5	8.3	8.6
	Public I/GDP	7.0	7.0	6.0	5.9	7.8	9.8	12.3	12.4	11.5	11.2	9.4	9.4	9.7	9.6	9.0	8.9	9.2	9.7	8.8	9.0	8.4	8.5	8.8	9.1	8.3	8.2	8.3	6.1	5.6	5.0	4.7
Panama	GDFI/GDP																15.4	17.0	19.3	8.8	6.5	8.5	15.0	18.5	23.2	23.6	26.0	25.3	26.5	28.1	29.6	29.9
	Private I/GDP																11.8	13.4	16.8	5.7	4.5	7.4	12.0	15.1	19.2	20.8	21.8	21.2	22.3	23.2	26.3	26.4
	Public I/GDP																3.7	3.7	2.4	3.1	2.0	1.1	3.0	3.4	4.0	2.9	4.3	4.0	4.2	4.8	3.3	3.5
Papua N. Guinea	GDFI/GDP												26.8	33.0	29.7	23.9	18.4	19.3	19.3	23.3	26.0	25.1	28.0	23.8	22.0	14.5	19.4	27.9	27.1	30.3		
	Private I/GDP												18.1	26.1	23.6	17.6	12.1	14.5	14.0	18.3	21.2	20.0	23.3	18.6	18.8	11.6	15.7	24.2	21.6	23.3		
	Public I/GDP												8.7	6.9	6.1	6.2	6.3	6.4	5.3	5.0	4.7	5.1	4.7	5.2	6.3	2.8	3.6	3.7	5.4	6.9		
Paraguay	GDFI/GDP	14.8	14.0	15.5	15.6	17.9	19.9	22.7	23.8	25.2	27.0	30.2	30.2	24.0	20.1	21.6	20.7	23.5	23.7	23.1	22.7	22.0	23.7	21.9	22.0	22.5	23.1	22.6	22.7	22.1	22.1	22.1
	Private I/GDP	10.8	10.3	11.0	12.3	15.2	15.7	13.5	15.2	17.9	20.7	25.7	25.7	22.7	13.3	13.2	14.2	18.5	17.6	16.3	16.0	19.2	20.4	18.2	18.8	19.0	17.7	18.2	15.2	14.4	14.2	14.2
	Public I/GDP	4.0	3.7	4.5	3.3	2.7	4.2	9.2	8.6	7.3	6.3	4.5	4.5	1.3	6.9	8.4	6.5	5.1	6.1	6.9	6.7	2.8	3.3	3.7	3.2	3.5	5.3	4.4	7.5	7.7	7.9	7.9
Peru	GDFI/GDP											28.8	28.8	29.5	23.7	20.2	18.2	18.5	17.8	19.7	16.6	16.1	16.6	16.5	18.3	21.2	24.3	22.6	24.0	23.8	21.6	21.4
	Private I/GDP											21.5	20.8	20.8	15.1	12.1	12.0	13.2	13.4	15.5	13.1	12.9	13.1	12.4	13.7	16.4	19.5	18.3	19.6	19.4	16.8	17.0
	Public I/GDP											7.3	8.7	8.7	8.6	8.1	6.1	5.4	4.4	4.2	3.5	3.2	3.5	4.1	4.7	4.8	4.7	4.3	4.4	4.5	4.8	4.4

Continued

TABLE C1. INVESTMENT AS A SHARE OF GDP (IN %) (Continued)

Country/Year		1970	1971	1972	1973	1974	1975	1976	1977	1978	1979	1980	1981	1982	1983	1984	1985	1986	1987	1988	1989	1990	1991	1992	1993	1994	1995	1996	1997	1998	1999	2000
Philippines	GDFI/GDP						24.7	26.4	25.1	25.2	27.5	27.2	27.8	27.5	29.8	24.5	17.5	16.8	16.5	17.8	20.8	23.1	20.0	20.9	23.8	24.3	22.0	23.6	25.1	20.2	18.6	17.6
	Private I/GDP						20.6	16.1	17.9	18.2	20.1	18.8	16.8	20.0	23.7	19.1	13.7	14.0	13.7	14.9	17.3	18.9	15.9	16.0	18.8	19.4	17.7	19.2	20.1	15.3	12.9	12.2
	Public I/GDP						4.1	10.3	7.2	7.0	7.4	8.5	10.9	7.5	6.1	5.4	3.7	2.8	2.8	2.9	3.6	4.2	4.1	4.9	5.0	4.9	4.3	4.4	5.0	4.9	5.7	5.4
Poland	GDFI/GDP																				16.0	20.7	20.9	17.5	15.9	15.1	15.4	17.0	19.3	20.4	20.5	20.1
	Private I/GDP																				2.7	8.5	12.3	7.7	6.4	6.7	6.8	7.8	10.3	11.8	12.7	12.8
	Public I/GDP																				13.3	12.1	8.5	9.8	9.4	8.5	8.6	9.2	9.0	8.6	7.8	7.4
Romania	GDFI/GDP																						14.2	14.7	14.1	16.1	18.0	19.2	17.4	16.4	16.4	13.5
	Private I/GDP																							1.4	2.3	3.7	5.9	7.1	7.6	6.2	6.6	6.9
	Public I/GDP																							12.9	12.4	10.4	10.2	10.9	11.6	11.3	9.8	6.6
Seychelles	GDFI/GDP																					23.0	21.3	21.0	26.8	24.7	30.3	49.1	30.7	38.0	37.1	29.3
	Private I/GDP																					14.8	8.4	11.5	15.6	17.1	23.6	41.0	21.9	24.6	24.8	17.3
	Public I/GDP																					8.2	12.9	9.4	11.2	7.5	6.8	8.1	8.9	13.4	12.3	12.0
South Africa	GDFI/GDP	24.7	26.2	26.9	25.4	25.1	29.4	30.1	28.0	26.4	26.2	26.2	27.8	27.9	26.8	24.4	23.3	20.2	18.5	19.8	20.6	19.6	17.2	15.7	14.7	15.2	15.9	16.1	16.3	16.5	14.9	
	Private I/GDP	14.1	14.5	14.0	13.5	13.4	14.8	14.7	13.7	13.0	12.7	13.3	15.5	15.9	15.6	14.6	13.1	11.6	11.2	13.2	13.2	12.9	11.0	10.4	10.3	11.0	11.6	11.7	11.8	11.1	10.3	
	Public I/GDP	10.6	11.7	12.8	11.9	11.7	14.6	15.5	14.3	13.4	13.5	12.9	12.3	12.0	11.2	9.9	10.2	8.6	7.3	6.7	7.4	6.8	6.1	5.2	4.4	4.1	4.3	4.4	4.5	5.4	4.6	
St. Lucia	GDFI/GDP											34.3	34.2	33.5	21.7	19.6	24.1	24.6	24.5	29.9	34.6	25.8	25.3	24.1	24.8	23.9	18.7	21.4	24.6	23.9	26.4	24.6
	Private I/GDP											25.1	26.1	24.7	13.0	12.3	15.7	14.6	14.1	16.8	20.7	13.8	12.0	10.6	11.6	12.3	10.4	14.6	18.2	15.5	16.9	15.8
	Public I/GDP											9.2	8.1	8.8	8.7	7.3	8.4	10.0	10.4	13.1	13.9	12.0	13.3	13.5	13.2	11.6	8.3	6.8	6.4	8.4	9.5	8.8
St. Vincent	GDFI/GDP																					26.2	29.7	29.4	24.3	25.6	28.2	30.2	28.3	29.7	31.8	32.6
	Private I/GDP																					14.6	18.1	17.5	11.3	16.0	16.0	24.2	21.4	17.5	18.1	18.8
	Public I/GDP																					11.6	11.6	12.0	13.0	9.9	12.2	6.0	6.9	12.2	13.8	13.8
Thailand	GDFI/GDP	23.8	23.3	22.7	22.4	23.3	22.9	22.9	26.0	25.3	25.6	27.8	28.0	26.9	28.5	28.6	27.2	25.8	27.6	30.7	34.6	40.4	41.6	39.3	39.5	39.9	40.9	41.0	33.8	29.0	28.7	26.6
	Private I/GDP	16.7	16.6	16.0	17.3	19.6	17.7	16.1	18.6	17.6	18.0	18.9	19.0	19.1	20.5	20.3	18.5	18.4	21.7	25.6	29.6	34.2	34.4	31.1	31.6	31.2	32.0	30.8	22.2	19.4	19.4	18.5
	Public I/GDP	7.1	6.7	6.7	5.1	3.7	5.2	6.8	7.4	7.7	7.6	8.8	8.9	7.9	8.0	8.3	8.7	7.4	6.0	5.0	5.0	6.1	7.2	8.1	7.9	8.7	8.9	10.2	11.6	9.6	9.3	8.1
Trinidad & Tobago	GDFI/GDP															26.1	18.8	21.6	19.3	13.1	16.6	12.6	16.6	14.1	14.3	20.2	20.8	24.3	36.1	28.0	21.0	21.8
	Private I/GDP															19.6	13.6	19.4	17.0	11.4	14.7	10.7	10.7	8.6	9.6	15.2	17.3	19.9	30.1	22.3	14.2	16.3
	Public I/GDP															6.4	5.2	2.2	2.4	1.7	1.9	1.9	6.0	5.5	4.8	5.0	3.5	4.4	5.9	5.7	6.7	5.5
Tunisia	GDFI/GDP	20.4	19.8	19.8	20.5	20.8	25.7	29.0	30.7	30.9	30.5	28.3	31.0	34.0	31.8	32.1	28.1	25.0	21.6	20.5	22.5	30.7	30.1	32.3	28.1	27.0	24.2	23.2	24.7	24.7	25.2	
	Private I/GDP	8.5	7.7	8.8	10.7	10.5	12.3	11.6	10.9	11.7	12.0	13.3	14.8	15.4	15.9	15.7	13.3	12.1	11.3	11.5	12.5	19.7	19.9	20.3	12.8	13.3	11.9	11.9	12.7	13.2	13.1	
	Public I/GDP	11.9	12.1	11.0	9.8	10.3	13.4	17.4	19.8	19.2	18.5	15.0	16.2	18.6	16.0	16.4	14.8	12.8	10.4	9.0	10.0	11.0	10.2	12.0	15.3	13.7	12.3	11.3	11.9	11.6	12.0	
Turkey	GDFI/GDP	22.5	20.2	21.7	21.4	19.9	22.1	24.4	25.7	23.1	21.9	22.1	20.1	19.4	20.1	19.5	20.3	22.8	24.7	26.1	22.8	22.9	23.7	23.0	25.5	24.5	24.2	25.4	26.8	24.9	22.3	23.8
	Private I/GDP	12.6	11.6	13.0	12.9	11.3	11.7	13.2	13.2	12.4	10.7	13.3	11.0	11.1	11.4	11.4	11.1	12.6	14.7	17.2	15.2	15.8	16.1	15.6	18.3	19.4	20.0	20.2	20.6	18.8	16.1	17.0
	Public I/GDP	9.9	8.6	8.7	8.5	8.6	10.4	11.2	12.5	10.7	11.2	8.8	9.2	8.3	8.7	8.1	9.2	10.2	10.0	8.9	7.6	7.0	7.6	7.4	7.3	5.0	4.2	5.2	6.2	6.1	6.2	6.8
Uruguay	GDFI/GDP	11.8	11.5	9.8	9.0	10.3	13.3	15.5	15.2	16.0	16.2	16.7	16.1	15.2	13.7	10.9	9.6	9.9	11.4	12.5	13.0	12.1	13.4	14.2	14.8	14.5	13.5	14.0	14.3	14.9	14.6	15.7
	Private I/GDP	8.8	8.3	7.5	7.1	7.7	8.7	9.0	8.2	8.0	9.7	11.9	10.9	8.0	8.6	6.4	6.1	6.2	7.4	7.6	8.4	8.3	9.3	9.9	10.3	10.1	9.9	10.5	10.6	10.9	10.6	12.1
	Public I/GDP	3.0	3.2	2.3	1.9	2.6	4.6	6.5	7.0	8.0	6.5	4.9	5.2	7.3	5.1	4.5	3.5	3.7	4.0	4.9	4.5	3.9	4.2	4.3	4.4	4.4	3.7	3.5	3.6	4.0	4.0	3.6

TABLE C1. INVESTMENT AS A SHARE OF GDP (IN %) (Continued)

Country/Year		1970	1971	1972	1973	1974	1975	1976	1977	1978	1979	1980	1981	1982	1983	1984	1985	1986	1987	1988	1989	1990	1991	1992	1993	1994	1995	1996	1997	1998	1999	2000
Uzbekistan	GDFI/GDP																									26.2	33.0	36.8	33.8	30.4	28.6	21.8
	Private I/GDP																									8.3	14.8	10.0	10.9	12.3	9.7	7.5
	Public I/GDP																									17.9	18.2	26.7	22.9	18.0	18.9	14.3
Venezuela, R. B.	GDFI/GDP															16.0	17.3	20.4	21.2	22.8	16.9	14.1	18.2	21.1	20.0	17.6	16.5	15.8	18.7	19.0	15.7	14.5
	Private I/GDP															10.5	11.1	10.9	12.1	12.3	7.2	4.9	7.6	8.9	9.0	8.2	7.1	7.0	9.4	10.7	8.8	8.4
	Public I/GDP															5.5	6.2	9.5	9.1	10.5	9.7	9.2	10.6	12.2	11.0	9.4	9.4	8.8	9.4	8.4	6.9	6.2
Yugoslavia, F.R.	GDFI/GDP																													11.2	13.0	15.4
	Private I/GDP																													9.8	11.4	13.1
	Public I/GDP																													1.4	1.6	2.3
East Asia	GDFI/GDP	21.3	22.3	22.2	23.1	25.1	24.8	24.1	25.5	26.5	28.0	27.7	27.2	29.4	28.9	26.5	24.8	24.7	24.6	24.1	25.9	27.5	28.2	28.1	28.7	28.8	29.8	31.1	29.9	26.2	24.4	22.0
	Private I/GDP	14.8	15.9	15.3	17.6	19.9	18.7	16.3	18.1	19.2	20.6	17.3	16.4	18.8	18.7	17.0	15.2	15.9	16.7	17.1	19.0	20.3	20.9	19.6	19.3	20.2	21.4	22.9	21.4	17.3	15.0	13.8
	Public I/GDP	6.6	6.4	6.9	5.5	5.2	6.1	7.8	7.4	7.2	7.4	10.4	10.8	10.6	10.2	9.5	9.5	8.8	7.9	7.0	6.9	7.2	7.4	8.5	9.4	8.6	8.4	8.2	8.5	9.0	9.4	8.2
South Asia	GDFI/GDP	14.1	14.3	13.9	9.5	11.2	12.3	15.1	15.6	15.5	15.4	17.0	19.9	19.6	18.5	18.0	18.7	18.9	19.3	18.8	19.6	19.1	18.8	19.5	19.5	19.4	20.1	20.1	19.6	19.3	18.9	17.9
	Private I/GDP	7.9	7.8	7.4	5.4	5.7	5.7	6.8	6.8	7.0	6.9	8.7	10.5	9.6	8.9	9.0	10.3	9.8	10.2	10.4	11.1	10.9	10.7	11.5	11.7	11.5	12.6	12.9	13.1	13.2	12.9	12.2
	Public I/GDP	6.2	6.5	6.5	4.1	5.5	6.6	8.3	8.8	8.5	8.4	8.3	9.4	10.0	9.6	9.0	8.5	9.1	9.1	8.4	8.5	8.2	8.1	8.0	7.9	7.9	7.6	7.2	6.5	6.1	6.0	5.7
LAC	GDFI/GDP	16.6	16.9	17.4	16.7	19.0	20.5	21.1	20.5	20.9	21.9	22.4	24.0	22.2	18.9	18.8	17.9	18.5	19.7	19.6	20.5	20.0	20.4	20.0	21.1	20.6	20.8	20.7	22.5	22.8	22.5	22.3
	Private I/GDP	11.5	11.6	11.5	11.1	12.5	13.2	13.1	12.8	13.3	13.1	14.5	15.0	13.5	10.9	11.6	11.4	12.1	13.4	12.8	13.7	13.3	13.4	13.1	14.3	14.1	14.4	13.9	15.5	16.1	15.1	15.9
	Public I/GDP	5.1	5.3	6.0	5.6	6.5	7.3	8.0	7.7	7.6	8.8	7.9	9.0	8.7	8.0	7.2	6.5	6.5	6.3	6.8	6.7	6.7	7.0	6.9	6.7	6.5	6.4	6.8	7.0	6.7	7.2	6.4
SSAFR	GDFI/GDP	22.2	24.4	22.2	22.2	21.1	24.8	25.2	24.7	27.7	25.6	24.5	23.2	20.5	19.0	17.7	17.2	17.0	19.2	21.8	20.1	19.0	18.3	20.0	19.0	19.1	19.0	20.2	18.5	18.6	19.0	19.3
	Private I/GDP	13.9	14.2	13.8	10.9	10.4	11.4	13.8	13.5	14.8	12.7	11.5	11.6	10.3	10.1	9.3	9.3	9.5	9.5	11.5	10.5	10.4	9.6	10.3	9.7	9.7	10.9	12.2	10.7	10.9	11.3	10.6
	Public I/GDP	8.3	10.2	10.7	11.3	10.7	13.4	11.4	11.2	12.9	12.9	13.0	11.7	10.2	8.9	8.4	7.8	7.4	9.7	10.3	9.7	8.6	8.7	9.8	9.2	9.4	8.1	8.0	7.9	7.7	7.7	8.7
ECA	GDFI/GDP	22.5	20.2	21.7	21.4	19.9	22.1	24.4	25.7	23.1	21.9	22.1	20.1	19.4	20.1	19.5	20.3	22.8	24.7	26.1	19.4	21.6	19.2	19.7	19.1	20.6	21.4	24.0	24.2	22.8	21.0	22.6
	Private I/GDP	12.6	11.6	13.0	12.9	11.3	11.7	13.2	13.2	12.4	10.7	13.3	11.0	11.1	11.4	11.4	11.1	12.6	14.7	17.2	8.9	8.4	7.6	10.3	11.1	11.5	12.5	14.1	15.7	15.9	14.3	16.2
	Public I/GDP	9.9	8.6	8.7	8.5	8.6	10.4	11.2	12.5	10.7	11.2	8.8	9.2	8.3	8.7	8.1	9.2	10.2	10.0	8.9	10.4	13.2	11.7	9.4	8.0	9.0	8.9	9.9	8.5	6.8	6.8	6.4
MENA	GDFI/GDP	20.4	19.8	19.8	20.5	20.8	25.3	29.3	31.3	27.9	27.2	24.1	25.3	27.2	28.0	27.1	25.2	24.0	20.6	21.9	22.3	24.6	24.2	24.1	22.3	21.8	21.2	21.1	22.0	22.2	22.9	24.7
	Private I/GDP	8.5	7.7	8.8	10.7	10.5	11.1	12.3	12.7	12.6	11.7	12.2	11.8	11.3	13.4	13.1	12.2	11.5	11.5	12.6	13.5	15.3	14.8	14.3	11.1	11.8	11.9	12.3	13.1	13.6	14.1	16.4
	Public I/GDP	11.9	12.1	11.0	9.8	10.3	14.2	17.1	18.6	15.3	15.6	11.9	13.5	15.9	14.6	14.0	13.0	12.5	9.1	9.3	8.8	9.3	9.4	9.8	11.2	10.1	9.3	8.8	8.8	8.5	8.8	8.3

Continued

TABLE C1. INVESTMENT AS A SHARE OF GDP (IN %) (Continued)

Country/Year	1970	1971	1972	1973	1974	1975	1976	1977	1978	1979	1980	1981	1982	1983	1984	1985	1986	1987	1988	1989	1990	1991	1992	1993	1994	1995	1996	1997	1998	1999	2000
Total GDFI/GDP	17.9	18.4	18.7	17.6	19.2	21.1	22.2	22.2	22.6	23.0	23.2	24.2	23.6	21.7	20.8	19.7	19.8	20.5	21.0	21.3	21.2	21.2	21.4	21.5	21.4	21.7	22.4	22.7	22.2	21.7	21.7
Total Private I/GDP	11.6	11.9	11.8	11.2	12.2	12.8	12.9	13.0	13.6	13.3	13.7	14.1	13.5	12.4	12.2	11.7	12.0	12.8	13.2	13.6	13.4	13.2	13.2	13.4	13.5	14.1	14.6	15.1	15.0	14.1	14.7
Total Public I/GDP	6.3	6.5	6.9	6.4	7.0	8.4	9.3	9.1	9.0	9.7	9.5	10.1	10.1	9.4	8.6	8.0	7.8	7.6	7.8	7.7	7.8	8.0	8.2	8.1	7.9	7.6	7.8	7.7	7.3	7.5	7.1

Notes:

– Unless otherwise noted the sources are: national authorities & World Bank/IMF staff estimates.

– Data for 1998/99 are preliminary/estimates.

– Azerbaijan: public investment includes mostly government investment as investment by state owned units is considered negligible.

– China: private investment includes: investment by collective-owned units, joint-owned units, share-holding units, foreign-funded units, Hong Kong-Macao-Taiwan-funded units and by individuals.

– Costa Rica: due to the revisions of the National Accounts methodology data for private, public investments are unavailable for 1999.

– Brazil: *source*–1990-1998: FIBGE e Centro de Estudos de Economia e Governo/IBRE/FGV, previous years World Bank.
Private investment includes investment by enterprises controlled by state and local municipalities for the period 1990-98.

– Kazakhstan: public investment includes mostly government investment as investment by state owned units is considered negligible.

– Korea, Republic of: *source*–Economic Statistics Yearbook various issues.

– Mauritania: 1999 private investment data are not available.

– Mexico: 1988-99 data based on a new INEGI methodology.

– Morocco: up to 1990 public investment are estimated by investment of 14 biggest public companies; 1990-1999 data for the whole economy.

– Papua New Guinea: 1999 data are unavailable.

– South Africa: *source*–Quarterly Bulletin of South African Reserve Bank.

Distributors of World Bank Group Publications

Prices and credit terms vary from country to country. Consult your local distributor before placing an order.

ARGENTINA
World Publications SA
Av. Cordoba 1877
1120 Ciudad de Buenos Aires
Tel: (54 11) 4815-8156
Fax: (54 11) 4815-8156
E-mail: wpbooks@infovia.com.ar

AUSTRALIA, FIJI, PAPUA NEW GUINEA, SOLOMON ISLANDS, VANUATU, AND SAMOA
D.A. Information Services
648 Whitehorse Road
Mitcham 3132, Victoria
Tel: (61) 3 9210 7777
Fax: (61) 3 9210 7788
E-mail: service@dadirect.com.au
URL: http://www.dadirect.com.au

AUSTRIA
Gerold and Co.
Weihburggasse 26
A-1011 Wien
Tel: (43 1) 512-47-31-0
Fax: (43 1) 512-47-31-29
URL: http://www.gerold.co/at.online

BANGLADESH
Micro Industries Development
Assistance Society (MIDAS)
House 5, Road 16
Dhanmondi R/Area
Dhzka 1209
Tel: (880 2) 326427
Fax: (880 2) 811188

BELGIUM
Jean De Lannoy
Av. du Roi 202
1060 Brussels
Tel: (32 2) 538-5169
Fax: (32 2) 538-0841

BRAZIL
Publicacões Tecnicas Internacionais
Ltda.
Rua Peixoto Gomide, 209
01409 Sao Paulo, SP.
Tel: (55 11) 259-6644
Fax: (55 11) 258-6990
E-mail: postmaster@pti.uol.br
URL: http://www.uol.br

CANADA
Renouf Publishing Co. Ltd.
5369 Canotek Road
Ottawa, Ontario K1J 9J3
Tel: (613) 745-2665
Fax: (613) 745-7660
E-mail:
   order.dept@renoufbooks.com
URL: http://www.renoufbooks.com

CHINA
China Financial & Economic
Publishing House
8, Da Fo Si Dong Jie
Beijing
Tel: (86 10) 6401-7365
Fax: (86 10) 6401-7365

China Book Import Centre
P.O. Box 2825
Beijing

Chinese Corporation for Promotion
of Humanities
52, You Fang Hu Tong,
Xuan Nei Da Jie
Beijing
Tel: (86 10) 660 72 494
Fax: (86 10) 660 72 494

COLOMBIA
Infoenlace Ltda.
Carrera 6 No. 51-21
Apartado Aereo 34270
Santafé de Bogotá, D.C.
Tel: (57 1) 285-2798
Fax: (57 1) 285-2798

COTE D'IVOIRE
Center d'Edition et de Diffusion
Africaines (CEDA)
04 B.P. 541
Abidjan 04
Tel: (225) 24 6510; 24 6511
Fax: (225) 25 0567

CYPRUS
Center for Applied Research
Cyprus College
6, Diogenes Street, Engomi
P.O. Box 2006
Nicosia
Tel: (357 2) 59-0730
Fax: (357 2) 66-2051

CZECH REPUBLIC
USIS, NIS Prodejna
Havelkova 22
130 00 Prague 3
Tel: (420 2) 2423 1486
Fax: (420 2) 2423 1114
URL: http://www.nis.cz/

DENMARK
SamfundsLitteratur
Rosenoerns Allé 11
DK-1970 Frederiksberg C
Tel: (45 35) 351942
Fax: (45 35) 357822
URL: http://www.sl.cbs.dk

ECUADOR
Libri Mundi
Libreria Internacional
P.O. Box 17-01-3029
Juan Leon Mera 851
Quito
Tel: (593 2) 521-606; (593 2) 544-185
Fax: (593 2) 504-209
E-mail: librimu1@librimundi.com.ec
E-mail: librimu2@librimundi.com.ec

CODEU
Ruiz de Castilla 763, Edif. Expocolor
Primer piso, Of. #2
Quito
Tel/Fax: (593 2) 507-383; 253-091
E-mail: codeu@impsat.net.ec

EGYPT, ARAB REPUBLIC OF
Al Ahram Distribution Agency
Al Galaa Street
Cairo
Tel: (20 2) 578-6083
Fax: (20 2) 578-6833

The Middle East Observer
41, Sherif Street
Cairo
Tel: (20 2) 393-9732
Fax: (20 2) 393-9732

FINLAND
Akateeminen Kirjakauppa
P.O. Box 128
FIN-00101 Helsinki
Tel: (358 0) 121 4418
Fax: (358 0) 121-4435
E-mail: akatilaus@stockmann.fi
URL: http://www.akateeminen.com

FRANCE
Editions Eska; DBJ
48, rue Gay Lussac
75005 Paris
Tel: (33-1) 55-42-73-08
Fax: (33-1) 43-29-91-67

GERMANY
UNO-Verlag
Poppelsdorfer Allee 55
53115 Bonn
Tel: (49 228) 949020
Fax: (49 228) 217492
URL: http://www.uno-verlag.de
E-mail: unoverlag@aol.com

GHANA
Epp Books Services
P.O. Box 44
TUC
Accra
Tel: 223 21 778843
Fax: 223 21 779099

GREECE
Papasotiriou S.A.
35, Stournara Str.
106 82 Athens
Tel: (30 1) 364-1826
Fax: (30 1) 364-8254

HAITI
Culture Diffusion
5, Rue Capois
C.P. 257
Port-au-Prince
Tel: (509) 23 9260
Fax: (509) 23 4858

HONG KONG, CHINA; MACAO
Asia 2000 Ltd.
Sales & Circulation Department
302 Seabird House
22-28 Wyndham Street, Central
Hong Kong, China
Tel: (852) 2530-1409
Fax: (852) 2526-1107
E-mail: sales@asia2000.com.hk
URL: http://www.asia2000.com.hk

HUNGARY
Euro Info Service
Margitszgeti Europa Haz
H-1138 Budapest
Tel: (36 1) 350 80 24, 350 80 25
Fax: (36 1) 350 90 32
E-mail: euroinfo@mail.matav.hu

INDIA
Allied Publishers Ltd.
751 Mount Road
Madras - 600 002
Tel: (91 44) 852-3938
Fax: (91 44) 852-0649

INDONESIA
Pt. Indira Limited
Jalan Borobudur 20
P.O. Box 181
Jakarta 10320
Tel: (62 21) 390-4290
Fax: (62 21) 390-4289

IRAN
Ketab Sara Co. Publishers
Khaled Eslamboli Ave., 6th Street
Delafrooz Alley No. 8
P.O. Box 15745-733
Tehran 15117
Tel: (98 21) 8717819; 8716104
Fax: (98 21) 8712479
E-mail: ketab-sara@neda.net.ir

Kowkab Publishers
P.O. Box 19575-511
Tehran
Tel: (98 21) 258-3723
Fax: (98 21) 258-3723

IRELAND
Government Supplies Agency
Oifig an tSoláthair
4-5 Harcourt Road
Dublin 2
Tel: (353 1) 661-3111
Fax: (353 1) 475-2670

ISRAEL
Yozmot Literature Ltd.
P.O. Box 56055
3 Yohanan Hasandlar Street
Tel Aviv 61560
Tel: (972 3) 5285-397
Fax: (972 3) 5285-397

R.O.Y. International
PO Box 13056
Tel Aviv 61130
Tel: (972 3) 649 9469
Fax: (972 3) 648 6039
E-mail: royil@netvision.net.il
URL: http://www.royint.co.il

Palestinian Authority/Middle East
Index Information Services
P.O.B. 19502 Jerusalem
Tel: (972 2) 6271219
Fax: (972 2) 6271634

ITALY, LIBERIA
Licosa Commissionaria Sansoni SPA
Via Duca Di Calabria, 1/1
Casella Postale 552
50125 Firenze
Tel: (39 55) 645-415
Fax: (39 55) 641-257
E-mail: licosa@ftbcc.it
URL: http://www.ftbcc.it/licosa

JAMAICA
Ian Randle Publishers Ltd.
206 Old Hope Road, Kingston 6
Tel: 876-927-2085
Fax: 876-977-0243
E-mail: irpl@colis.com

JAPAN
Eastern Book Service
3-13 Hongo 3-chome, Bunkyo-ku
Tokyo 113
Tel: (81 3) 3818-0861
Fax: (81 3) 3818-0864
E-mail: orders@svt-ebs.co.jp
URL:
   http://www.bekkoame.or.jp/~svt-ebs

KENYA
Africa Book Service (E.A.) Ltd.
Quaran House, Mfangano Street
P.O. Box 45245
Nairobi
Tel: (254 2) 223 641
Fax: (254 2) 330 272

Legacy Books
Loita House
Mezzanine 1
P.O. Box 68077
Nairobi
Tel: (254) 2-330853, 221426
Fax: (254) 2-330854, 561654
E-mail: Legacy@form-net.com

KOREA, REPUBLIC OF
Dayang Books Trading Co.
International Division
783-20, Pangba Bon-Dong,
Socho-ku
Seoul
Tel: (82 2) 536-9555
Fax: (82 2) 536-0025
E-mail: seamap@chollian.net

Eulyoo Publishing Co., Ltd.
46-1, Susong-Dong
Jongro-Gu
Seoul
Tel: (82 2) 734-3515
Fax: (82 2) 732-9154

LEBANON
Librairie du Liban
P.O. Box 11-9232
Beirut
Tel: (961 9) 217 944
Fax: (961 9) 217 434
E-mail: hsayegh@librairie-du-liban.com.lb
URL: http://www.librairie-du-liban.com.lb

MALAYSIA
University of Malaya Cooperative
Bookshop, Limited
P.O. Box 1127
Jalan Pantai Baru
59700 Kuala Lumpur
Tel: (60 3) 756-5000
Fax: (60 3) 755-4424
E-mail: umkoop@tm.net.my

MEXICO
INFOTEC
Av. San Fernando No. 37
Col. Toriello Guerra
14050 Mexico, D.F.
Tel: (52 5) 624-2800
Fax: (52 5) 624-2822
E-mail: infotec@rtn.net.mx
URL: http://rtn.net.mx

Mundi-Prensa Mexico S.A. de C.V.
c/Rio Panuco, 141-Colonia
Cuauhtemoc
06500 Mexico, D.F.
Tel: (52 5) 533-5658
Fax: (52 5) 514-6799

NEPAL
Everest Media International Services
(P.) Ltd.
GPO Box 5443
Kathmandu
Tel: (977 1) 416 026
Fax: (977 1) 224 431

NETHERLANDS
De Lindeboom/Internationale
Publicaties b.v.-
P.O. Box 202, 7480 AE Haaksbergen
Tel: (31 53) 574-0004
Fax: (31 53) 572-9296
E-mail: lindeboo@worldonline.nl
URL: http://www.worldonline.nl/~lindeboo

NEW ZEALAND
EBSCO NZ Ltd.
Private Mail Bag 99914
New Market
Auckland
Tel: (64 9) 524-8119
Fax: (64 9) 524-8067

Oasis Official
P.O. Box 3627
Wellington
Tel: (64 4) 499 1551
Fax: (64 4) 499 1972
E-mail: oasis@actrix.gen.nz
URL: http://www.oasisbooks.co.nz/

NIGERIA
University Press Limited
Three Crowns Building Jericho
Private Mail Bag 5095
Ibadan
Tel: (234 22) 41-1356
Fax: (234 22) 41-2056

PAKISTAN
Mirza Book Agency
65, Shahrah-e-Quaid-e-Azam
Lahore 54000
Tel: (92 42) 735 3601
Fax: (92 42) 576 3714

Oxford University Press
5 Bangalore Town
Sharae Faisal
PO Box 13033
Karachi-75350
Tel: (92 21) 446307
Fax: (92 21) 4547640
E-mail: ouppak@TheOffice.net

Pak Book Corporation
Aziz Chambers 21, Queen's Road
Lahore
Tel: (92 42) 636 3222; 636 0885
Fax: (92 42) 636 2328
E-mail: pbc@brain.net.pk

PERU
Editorial Desarrollo SA
Apartado 3824, Ica 242 OF. 106
Lima 1
Tel: (51 14) 285380
Fax: (51 14) 286628

PHILIPPINES
International Booksource Center Inc.
1127-A Antipolo St, Barangay,
Venezuela
Makati City
Tel: (63 2) 896 6501; 6505; 6507
Fax: (63 2) 896 1741

POLAND
International Publishing Service
Ul. Piekna 31/37
00-677 Warzawa
Tel: (48 2) 628-6089
Fax: (48 2) 621-7255
E-mail: books%ips@ikp.atm.com.pl
URL:
   http://www.ipscg.waw.pl/ips/export

PORTUGAL
Livraria Portugal
Apartado 2681, Rua Do Carm
o 70-74
1200 Lisbon
Tel: (1) 347-4982
Fax: (1) 347-0264

ROMANIA
Compani De Librarii Bucuresti S.A.
Str. Lipscani no. 26, sector 3
Bucharest
Tel: (40 1) 313 9645
Fax: (40 1) 312 4000

RUSSIAN FEDERATION
Isdatelstvo <Ves Mir>
9a, Kolpachniy Pereulok
Moscow 101831
Tel: (7 095) 917 87 49
Fax: (7 095) 917 92 59
ozimarin@glasnet.ru

SINGAPORE; TAIWAN, CHINA MYANMAR; BRUNEI
Hemisphere Publication Services
41 Kallang Pudding Road #04-03
Golden Wheel Building
Singapore 349316
Tel: (65) 741-5166
Fax: (65) 742-9356
E-mail: ashgate@asianconnect.com

SLOVENIA
Gospodarski vestnik Publishing
Group
Dunajska cesta 5
1000 Ljubljana
Tel: (386 61) 133 83 47; 132 12 30
Fax: (386 61) 133 80 30
E-mail: repansekj@gvestnik.si

SOUTH AFRICA, BOTSWANA
For single titles:
Oxford University Press Southern
Africa
Vasco Boulevard, Goodwood
P.O. Box 12119, N1 City 7463
Cape Town
Tel: (27 21) 595 4400
Fax: (27 21) 595 4430
E-mail: oxford@oup.co.za

For subscription orders:
International Subscription Service
P.O. Box 41095
Craighall
Johannesburg 2024
Tel: (27 11) 880-1448
Fax: (27 11) 880-6248
E-mail: iss@is.co.za

SPAIN
Mundi-Prensa Libros, S.A.
Castello 37
28001 Madrid
Tel: (34 91) 4 363700
Fax: (34 91) 5 753998
E-mail: libreria@mundiprensa.es
URL: http://www.mundiprensa.com/

Mundi-Prensa Barcelona
Consell de Cent, 391
08009 Barcelona
Tel: (34 3) 488-3492
Fax: (34 3) 487-7659
E-mail: barcelona@mundiprensa.es

SRI LANKA, THE MALDIVES
Lake House Bookshop
100, Sir Chittampalam Gardiner
Mawatha
Colombo 2
Tel: (94 1) 32105
Fax: (94 1) 432104
E-mail: LHL@sri.lanka.net

SWEDEN
Wennergren-Williams AB
P. O. Box 1305
S-171 25 Solna
Tel: (46 8) 705-97-50
Fax: (46 8) 27-00-71
E-mail: mail@wwi.se

SWITZERLAND
Librairie Payot Service Institutionnel
C(tm)tes-de-Montbenon 30
1002 Lausanne
Tel: (41 21) 341-3229
Fax: (41 21) 341-3235

ADECO Van Diermen
EditionsTechniques
Ch. de Lacuez 41
CH1807 Blonay
Tel: (41 21) 943 2673
Fax: (41 21) 943 3605

THAILAND
Central Books Distribution
306 Silom Road
Bangkok 10500
Tel: (66 2) 2336930-9
Fax: (66 2) 237-8321

TRINIDAD & TOBAGO AND THE CARRIBBEAN
Systematics Studies Ltd.
St. Augustine Shopping Center
Eastern Main Road, St. Augustine
Trinidad & Tobago, West Indies
Tel: (868) 645-8466
Fax: (868) 645-8467
E-mail: tobe@trinidad.net

UGANDA
Gustro Ltd.
PO Box 9997, Madhvani Building
Plot 16/4 Jinja Rd.
Kampala
Tel: (256 41) 251 467
Fax: (256 41) 251 468
E-mail: gus@swiftuganda.com

UNITED KINGDOM
Microinfo Ltd.
P.O. Box 3, Omega Park, Alton,
Hampshire GU34 2PG
England
Tel: (44 1420) 86848
Fax: (44 1420) 89889
E-mail: wbank@microinfo.co.uk
URL: http://www.microinfo.co.uk

The Stationery Office
51 Nine Elms Lane
London SW8 5DR
Tel: (44 171) 873-8400
Fax: (44 171) 873-8242
URL: http://www.the-stationery-office.co.uk/

VENEZUELA
Tecni-Ciencia Libros, S.A.
Centro Cuidad Comercial Tamanco
Nivel C2, Caracas
Tel: (58 2) 959 5547; 5035; 0016
Fax: (58 2) 959 5636

ZAMBIA
University Bookshop, University of
Zambia
Great East Road Campus
P.O. Box 32379
Lusaka
Tel: (260 1) 252 576
Fax: (260 1) 253 952

ZIMBABWE
Academic and Baobab Books (Pvt.)
Ltd.
4 Conald Road, Graniteside
P.O. Box 567
Harare
Tel: 263 4 755035
Fax: 263 4 781913